How The Other Half Loves

A Comedy by
Alan Ayckbourn

Evans Plays London

HOW THE OTHER HALF LOVES

This play was presented by Peter Bridge at the Lyric Theatre, London, on 5th August, 1970, with the following cast:

FRANK FOSTER	Robert Morley
FIONA FOSTER	Joan Tetzel
BOB PHILLIPS	Donald Burton
TERRY PHILLIPS	Heather Sears
WILLIAM FEATHERSTONE	Brian Miller
MARY FEATHERSTONE	Elizabeth Ashton

Directed by	ROBIN MIDGLEY
Designed by	ALAN TAGG
Lighting by	JOHN B. READ

The action of this play takes place in the living rooms of the Fosters and Phillips.

ACT I

Scene One

The lights come up on the main set to reveal two living rooms. Not a composite setting but two rooms contained and overlapping in the same area. Only the furnishings themselves, both in colour and style indicate which belongs to which room.

The FOSTER's furniture is smart period reproduction, while the PHILLIPS' is more modern, trendy and badly looked after. Both rooms have similar items. D.R. is the PHILLIPS' dining table and two chairs. To L. of PHILLIPS' table is a three-seater settee with the R. two seats matching the FOSTER's decor and the L. seat matching the PHILLIPS' decor. C. is an armchair (FOSTER) and L. is another armchair (PHILLIPS). R. of C. chair is a small table (FOSTER). U.L. is the FOSTER's dining table and two chairs. D.C. is a composite coffee table with PHILLIPS' section R. and FOSTER's section L. On each section is a telephone. D.L. is the PHILLIPS' child's playpen and toys including a doll's house and the PHILLIPS' armchair.

Each room has two doors and a window as follows: D.R. PHILLIPS' window, R. FOSTER's kitchen door, U.R. PHILLIPS' front door, U.L. FOSTER's front double doors, L. PHILLIPS' kitchen and D.L. FOSTER's window.

It is early Thursday morning.

The FOSTER's main door opens and FIONA, an elegant woman in her forties, enters in her dressing gown. She goes to window L. and draws the curtains. The lights come up on the FOSTER's areas. She crosses to the phone and dials. The phone in the PHILLIPS' house starts to ring. After a second, TERESA, an untidy, rather intense, tired looking woman in her early thirties, enters from kitchen door carrying a mug of tea. She is in a different room to FIONA and so does not acknowledge her presence in any way. The characters in their different rooms will often pass extremely close but without ever actually touching. TERESA picks up her receiver.

TERESA	Hallo. Hallo ...
	(FIONA hangs up with a sigh. She looks at her watch. TERESA, frowning, crosses to her curtains R. and draws them. The lights come up on the PHILLIPS' areas. She reacts to the bright early morning light. She switches on her portable radio which is on the dining table. It is a news programme. FIONA, who has been standing thoughtfully, turns and goes out into the kitchen. TERESA sits, reading a newspaper cutting and drinking tea. The FOSTER's double doors fly open again and FRANK enters like a whirlwind. He is dressed in running shorts, a vest and a jaunty sporting cap and is breathing heavily. As he enters, the kitchen timer which is on the coffee table, rings. FRANK reaches it and it stops ringing. He surveys it in disgust and then switches on the radio on the coffee table. Loud military music. He picks up a skipping rope from the coffee table and with an effort, starts to skip. After a moment, FIONA re-enters. She takes in FRANK with a frown, goes to the coffee table and, almost unconsciously, switches the radio off.)
FIONA	That's rather grotesque, darling. Do you have to do that first thing in the morning? I'm sure you'll damage yourself one of these days. It's twenty past. Did you know?
FRANK	That's rather why I switched the radio on. (He sits on chair C.)
FIONA	(without pausing on her way out) Alright. So long as you know. (She goes out into the hall.)
TERESA	(crossing to the bedroom door and calling) Bob! Bob! It's twenty five past - Bob! Get up! (She gives up

after hearing no reply and goes out L.)

(FIONA enters immediately with the newspapers which she tosses on to the settee.)

FIONA Frank, I'll have to have the car this morning –

FRANK Oh yes?

FIONA I've got an awful lot of dashing around to do.

FRANK Well, you – haven't got to dash around this morning, have you?

FIONA I have to dash around every morning, darling, but this is more frantic than usual –

FRANK It's jolly inconvenient, as it happens –

FIONA Yes, it's jolly inconvenient for both of us, darling. But I just can't manage without it –

FRANK (picking up phone and starting to dial) As long as that's perfectly clear. I mean you're not the only one that has to dash around, you know. I mean there are times when I'm – dashing around –

FIONA Yes, well, I'll get us some breakfast. You ought to get dressed. (She goes out into the kitchen.)

(The PHILLIPS' phone rings.)

FRANK (muttering) Quite frequently – dashing around –

(BOB, in his early thirties, enters blearily from kitchen. He answers the phone, having first switched off TERESA's radio.)

BOB Hallo.

FRANK (startled) Hallo. Who's this?

BOB What?

FRANK Who am I talking to?

BOB Good morning, Frank. This is Bob Phillips.

FRANK Ah, good morning Bob. I'm glad you rang, I wanted a word. I've asked everyone to get to the office a little earlier this morning. I tried to catch you yesterday.

	What happend to you? Sneak off a bit early, did you?
BOB	Yes I had – to meet someone ...
FRANK	Oh yes? I won't ask who. (He laughs.) (BOB laughs.) Listen Bob, can you be in by a quarter past?
BOB	I'll try.
FRANK	I'd like the whole team there. Full strength. Right?
BOB	Right. (He goes to hang up.)
FRANK	Oh, Bob –
BOB	Yes?
FRANK	Do you know anything about Featherstone?
BOB	Do I know about what?
FRANK	Featherstone. Bright little chap from Accounts. Do you know him at all?
BOB	Oh, William Featherstone. Yes.
FRANK	What's your opinion of him?
BOB	(surprised) He's alright.
FRANK	Good man, is he?
BOB	Fine – as far as I know.
FRANK	(hanging up) Good. Good. Good. (He rises, switches on his radio and goes out to the hall, muttering.) I'm frequently dashing around. (BOB is left holding the receiver for a moment. As TERESA enters from L. engrossed in the paper, her mug of tea still in her hand, he replaces the receiver.)
BOB	Morning.
TERESA	(without looking up) Hallo. (She sits on L. end of sofa.) Who was that?
BOB	Just business.
TERESA	Oh.

BOB	Any tea?
TERESA	Just made it.
BOB	Oh. Good.
TERESA	On the stove. My God, there's another letter from this woman – That's about three this week already –
BOB	On the stove?
TERESA	What?
BOB	The tea?
TERESA	That's right. Help yourself –
	(BOB breaks L. and turns back.)
	Oh no, honestly, that's incredible. She's raised six hundred pounds just in coffee mornings amongst her friends. Isn't that incredible?
BOB	(crossing to L. of TERESA) Perhaps you ought to do the same thing with tea mornings? Invite me along. That way I might even get a cup.
TERESA	It's on the stove –
BOB	Fine. Fine.
	(FIONA enters from kitchen R. with tray and crosses L. BOB crosses L. and goes into kitchen L. FIONA puts tray on table L. and begins to unload it.)
TERESA	(engrossed again in her newspaper) Oh – no! Honestly –
FRANK	(coming in through main door and crossing towards kitchen R.) Darling – Darling?
FIONA	Hallo?
FRANK	(crossing to R. of FIONA) It would appear that I have no clean shirt. Is that in fact the case?
FIONA	Hmm?
FRANK	No clean shirts. I have no clean shirts, apparently.
FIONA	Well, darling, if you'd like to pop upstairs again and look on the third shelf down, I think you'll find no less than

three shirts, all nice and clean and still wrapped up in cellophane bags from the laundry –

FRANK	Third shelf?
FIONA	That's right.
FRANK	What the devil are they doing on the third shelf?
FIONA	Presumably lying there, waiting for you to put them on, darling.
FRANK	What are they doing on the third shelf. What's wrong with the second shelf –
FIONA	Nothing at all as far as I know darling, but since nineteen fifty-seven your shirts have always been kept on the third shelf down. They have not been kept on the second shelf down since we moved from Woking.
FRANK	Woking?
FIONA	(crossing to kitchen door R.) We weren't so well off in Woking, if you remember. You had a smaller wardrobe –
FRANK	(crossing to U.C.) I don't know anything about Woking –
FIONA	(going out R. with the empty tray) You go and have a look –
FRANK	Why the hell does she have to drag Woking into the conversation – (He tramps out U.L.C., disgruntled.)
	(BOB enters from kitchen L. and crosses slowly to L. of TERESA.)
BOB	I see you're hanging on with grim nostalgia to that empty cornflake packet.
TERESA	Mmmm? Oh, that. I didn't have time.
BOB	Ah.
TERESA	Did you get your tea?
BOB	No. It appears you only made enough for one –
TERESA	No, I didn't –
BOB	That was the impression I got from the teapot, anyway. I

did toy with the idea of chewing the leaves but decided to make some fresh instead.   (He crosses to dresser U.R. for a cigarette.)

(FIONA enters from kitchen R. with a tray, crosses D.S. of BOB to table L. BOB crosses to U.S. of TERESA who closes the newspaper.)

TERESA	Is Benjamin awake?
BOB	Haven't heard him.
TERESA	He's marvellous these days. It used to be four o'clock, didn't it?
BOB	So I remember telling you at the time –
TERESA	I got up now and again, as well –
BOB	Now and again.
FIONA	(going out R., calling) Frank – breakfast –

(BOB goes to dresser for matches and FIONA crosses D.S. of him and goes out to kitchen R. BOB crosses to D.R. of sofa.)

TERESA	Did you want some breakfast, then? Is that what this is all about?
BOB	Not if – you're rushed off your feet.
TERESA	Well, there's no need to go on at me. I mean considering the fact that you rolled in here at two o'clock this morning stinking drunk and I haven't said a word about it –
BOB	Till now –
TERESA	Haven't said a word about it, I think it's really a bit of a nerve to sit there complaining there isn't any breakfast –
BOB	I'm not complaining.
TERESA	Good.

(BOB crosses L. and pauses L. of C. chair. FIONA enters from kitchen R. and crosses U.S. of BOB to table L. with egg and toast on tray.)

BOB	(going out L.) What on earth have I to complain about?

FIONA	Frank - it's on the table - (She goes to doors U.L.)
FRANK	(off) Coming -
	(FIONA goes to the phone and dials. TERESA's phone rings. TERESA answers it.)
TERESA	Hallo ....
FIONA	(is about to replace the phone when FRANK enters U.L., pulling on his jacket) ... eight twenty-eight and twenty seconds ... (She seems to adjust her watch.)
TERESA	What? Hallo?
	(FIONA replaces the receiver.)
	Hallo? (After a second she replaces the receiver, puzzled, and then resumes her reading.)
FIONA	(crossing to table L.) Eight twenty-eight and twenty seconds -
FRANK	(crossing to C. chair and moving small table from R. to front of C. chair) Is that what it is?
FIONA	Yes.
FRANK	Oh. Damn fool on the wireless has just said it's eight thirty-three - (He sits in armchair.)
	(FIONA picks up tray and crosses to L. of FRANK and put tray on his table, and then crosses back to table L. sits and pours coffee.)
FIONA	Well, they can't both be right -
FRANK	Hardly. Ah! (He tackles his egg.)
	(FIONA butters herself some toast, and pours coffee. BOB enters from kitchen L. and crosses to C. waves his mug at TERESA and then crosses and sits in armchair D.L.)
BOB	Benjamin's awake now.
TERESA	Is he crying?
BOB	No just beating on the floor with his wet nappy -
TERESA	Oh, well, I'll leave him for a minute. Get you your bloomin' breakfast -

BOB	As I say. Don't go out of your way –
TERESA	Oh, shut up. Some woman rang up just now.
BOB	Woman.
TERESA	Yes. Told me the time and rang off.
BOB	Tim's mother, do you think?
TERESA	Oh no, it wasn't that. Anyway, you're supposed to ring them, aren't you?
BOB	It's customary. Was she abusive as well – lewd suggestions?
TERESA	No. (She rises and drops newspaper R. of FRANK.) She was a couple of minutes fast –
BOB	No one I know.
TERESA	I didn't imagine it would be. (She goes out L.)

(FIONA rises, gives coffee to FRANK and then crosses R. and sits R. end of sofa with her coffee and reads a newspaper. BOB sips his tea. FRANK sniffs at his egg.)

FIONA	It's perfectly fresh.
FRANK	Just make sure. Always make sure first –
FIONA	Yes, I've noticed.
FRANK	Yes. This is fine. Good fresh egg this.
FIONA	Good.
FRANK	(eating) Very nice. Very nice indeed –

(BOB rises, crosses to C. and picks up newspaper and then sits again D.L. FIONA reads paper.)

Pity you couldn't get home till late last night.

FIONA	Oh? Why's that?
FRANK	Well, with being – er – well no point in it really. Sentimental. No, no, no –
FIONA	Being what?
FRANK	Oh, I don't know why. Always seem to get a bit gooey over these sort of things. I don't know why. It's the women who're supposed to be gooey, aren't they?

FIONA   Darling, gooey about what?

FRANK   Our wedding anniversary.

FIONA   (dead)   Oh, Lord.

FRANK   (laughing, embarrassed)   Silly, isn't it?

FIONA   Oh, Lord.

FRANK   No matter. I – er, bought some special plonk actually. You know, some of your – special plonk –

FIONA   Did you?

FRANK   Matter of fact I – drank the lot. Rather merry. Opened it up – let the air in and so forth – come eleven thirty – not a drop. Thought, well, if she walks in now, sees I've drunk all her special plonk – me for the doghouse, eh?

FIONA   I got held up, I'm afraid.

FRANK   Yes, I thought you'd been held up. Another meeting was it?

FIONA   Umm –

FRANK   No. It couldn't have been a meeting, because your Mrs Thingamejig rang up and said you weren't there and where were you, and I remember saying to her that I thought you must have been held up.

FIONA   Mrs Who?

FRANK   Can't remember offhand. Mrs Thingamejig –

FIONA   Oh, Lord.   (She continues to read the paper rather angrily.)

          (TERESA enters from kitchen L. and crosses to R. of BOB with sandwich on a plate.)

TERESA   I had to get Benjamin up. Put him in his chair. He's tearing the wallpaper up there. I think he's bored. We ought to find something to amuse him. Something on elastic he can twang. Amy Murchison gave her kid an old bra of hers and a couple of tennis balls. Kept it happy for hours. Bit Freudian, though, isn't it? Here you are. (She holds plate out to BOB.)

BOB	What's that? (He puts newspaper on floor.)
TERESA	(still holding out plate) Your breakfast. I made you a sandwich.
BOB	What sort of sandwich?
TERESA	Peanut butter.
BOB	(staring at it) Peanut butter?
TERESA	It's all we seem to have.
BOB	You shouldn't have gone to all this trouble, you know.
TERESA	(dropping plate and sandwich into BOB's lap almost casually) Don't have the damn thing, then. (She snatches up the paper and sits L. end of settee.)
	(BOB stares at the sandwich, thoughtfully. FRANK has finished his egg with a flourish and turns his attention to the toast.)
FRANK	This toast alright?
FIONA	Perfectly.
FRANK	Seems a bit dried out. Dry you know.
FIONA	I should damp it down then, darling, if I were you –
FRANK	(doubtfully) Um.
	(BOB rises and crosses to L. of Terry with the plate.)
BOB	Never mind. It was a beautiful thought.
TERESA	Don't you like peanut butter?
BOB	Not round about now I don't.
TERESA	That's funny. Benjamin adores it –
BOB	Does he?
TERESA	Yes. Out of a spoon. He can't get enough of it.
BOB	Well, I obviously don't take after Benjamin. I'll put it next to the cornflake packet. As a memento. (He crosses L. and turns back.) I don't know what you're reading that for. You've read one newspaper, you've read the lot. (He exits into kitchen L.) There's

	a report in there of this fellow's speech – exactly the same speech that was reported in yesterday's paper –
TERESA	This is yesterday's paper.
BOB	(appearing in kitchen doorway) Yesterday's?
TERESA	I hadn't finished reading it.
BOB	Well, where the hell's today's?
TERESA	I don't know. Outside, probably.
BOB	(going out L.) Oh my God –
TERESA	(calling after him) See Benjamin's alright, will you? (FIONA folds up the paper.)
FRANK	That toothbrush is on the blink by the way.
FIONA	Um?
FRANK	I'll have to look at it after breakfast. Electric toothbrush. On the blink.
FIONA	Oh, is it?
FRANK	Battery's flat by the sound of it. Hardly a flicker out of it.
FIONA	No?
FRANK	No. Had to clean my teeth with the flannel.
FIONA	Your own I hope.
FRANK	Oh yes. The blue one.
FIONA	That's the bath cloth.
FRANK	Ah! Is it? Is it! (He is thoughtful, sucking his teeth speculatively.)
BOB	(coming in from kitchen L. and crossing up to U.S. of table L.) Benjamin's poured his prunes all over his head –
TERESA	(leaping up) Oh no – (She drops paper and goes out into kitchen L.)
BOB	(following her) Perhaps he prefers peanut butter – (BOB and TERESA go out.)

FRANK	Where did you get to then?
FIONA	When?
FRANK	Last night?
FIONA	Oh, I got held up –
FRANK	Oh. (pause) I see. Doesn't matter.
FIONA	It's no secret. There's no secret about it.
FRANK	Isn't there?
FIONA	No. No secret at all. (She rises and crosses to R. of FRANK putting her cup on coffee table.)
FRANK	Good.
FIONA	More coffee? (She picks up tray and crosses to D.S. of table L. and pours coffee.)
FRANK	Ah, thank you.
	(BOB enters laughing from kitchen L. and crosses to U.R. of FRANK. TERESA follows him and crosses U.S. of BOB to table D.R.)
TERESA	I don't know what you think is so damn funny.
BOB	I think the prune juice suits him –
TERESA	(sourly) Oh ha-ha – (She grabs handful of tissues from box on table D.R. and crosses L.) You're no help. No help at all – (She goes out L.)
	(BOB turns and goes out U.R.)
FRANK	Oh that reminds me, I mustn't forget to give you your present.
FIONA	Present?
FRANK	Your anniversary present. I must give you that before I go.
FIONA	(crossing to L. of FRANK with coffee) There's no need to rub it in, darling.
FRANK	What? Oh. That wasn't my intention. Wasn't my intention to rub it in.
	(FIONA crosses D.S. of FRANK, collects her own cup

from coffee table and crosses U.S. to table L. BOB comes on U.R. with new newspaper and crosses D.S. to phone.)

FIONA   Good.

FRANK   Good Lord, no.

(TERESA enters from kitchen L. and crosses U.S. of BOB to wastepaper basket D.R. BOB drops phone and opens the paper.)

TERESA   Where the hell were you last night, anyway?

BOB   Me?

TERESA   Where were you?

(BOB crosses and sits in armchair D.L. FIONA crosses and sits R. end of sofa.)

BOB   What a funny question.

TERESA   (crossing U.S. to L. of sofa)   No, I'm sick of this. Other husbands tell their wives where they go to. They don't just disappear and come blundering in at two o'clock in the morning. Other husbands –   (She crosses to R. of BOB and pulls apron off back of armchair.)   I mean here am I stuck here with Benjamin and you're out having parties and God knows what else and here am I stuck here.

BOB   What's all this in aid of?   (He rises and crosses D.R., takes jacket from chair D.S. of table and puts it on.)

TERESA   He's your child as much as mine.

BOB   I believe you.

TERESA   (crossing D.S. to L. of C.)   Well, where were you? I want to know. Where were you?

BOB   (indignant)   Out.

TERESA   Just out?

BOB   (crossing to R. of TERESA)   That's right.

TERESA   What doing?

BOB   Drinking, talking –

TERESA	Who with?
BOB	Why do you want to know –
TERESA	Because I'm not a fool you know. I'm not a complete fool. I mean I'd be very stupid indeed if I didn't notice –

(A crash off.)

Oh no! Wait a minute.   (She hurries off L.)
Benjamin! Benjamin, you stop that at once –

(BOB meanders and sits L. end of sofa.)

FRANK	(rising and crossing U.S.) I think I will get it for you, though. All the same the present – (He goes out U.L.)

(FIONA rises and crosses to D.S. of table L. and puts down cup, dropping newspaper on C. chair on her way.)

FIONA	(annoyed with herself) Oh –

(TERESA enters from kitchen L. with large spoon and crosses to L. of BOB. FIONA crosses to L. of armchair C. and picks up papers.)

TERESA	I caught him trying to swallow this.
BOB	Really?
TERESA	He could have choked. Easily.
BOB	I think he'd have stood a good chance.
TERESA	You don't care. You don't care at all, do you? You don't care. You don't care about me, you don't care about Benjamin – (She crosses to armchair D.L. and throws spoon in playpen.) You just don't care. (She sits D.L.)

(Pause. FIONA sits C. chair.)

BOB	What is the matter with you.
TERESA	(more subdued) I don't think I can cope. I've just about had it. I don't think I can cope, any more.
BOB	You do alright.
TERESA	The house is in a mess. I'm in a mess. Benjamin's covered in prunes – Everything's foul.

BOB   (uselessly)   Never mind.

TERESA   Then I read the papers and I feel more useless. Do you
             know that woman who raised that six hundred pounds.
             She's got three children –

BOB   So what? She's probably got a staff of fifteen –

TERESA   Three children. Here's me with one and I can't cope.
             And she writes letters –

BOB   You write letters.

TERESA   Nobody ever publishes mine though. I mean there must be
             something I can do. Something worthwhile. Instead of
             just sitting here, on my own, like a – cow, or something.

             (Pause.)

             You're never here.

BOB   I'm always here –   Mostly.

TERESA   Not when I need you, you're not. Not when I want to
             talk.

             (They both sit gloomily in silence.)

FRANK   (re-entering U.L. and crossing to R. of FIONA with a
             small parcel done up with ribbon)   Here we are.
             (He puts it in front of FIONA.)   There. Open your
             mouth, shut your eyes and prepare yourself for a big
             surprise.   (He hands FIONA present.)

FIONA   Oh. Thank you, darling.   (She puts present down on
             table.)

FRANK   Well.   (He hands present back to FIONA.)
             Come on, then. Open it up.

FIONA   (beginning to open present)   Oh, alright. You do
             realise, I've totally forgotten to get you anything, don't
             you?

FRANK   Yes. That's alright. That's alright.

FIONA   Right.

TERESA   There must be someone I can help.

BOB   Who?

TERESA	Anyone.
FIONA	(pulling out a bottle of perfume from the parcel) Oh. How nice. How very nice. Thank you, darling. Very thoughtful.
FRANK	It's the sort you use, isn't it?
FIONA	No. Not really.
FRANK	Oh. (Pause.) Oh, I see.
FIONA	No, I don't usually wear this one, darling. What a lovely pretty bottle, though, isn't it?
FRANK	Well, I can change it. Change it.
FIONA	No, it's alright, darling. There's no need to bother. I'll just wear it round the house. That sort of thing.
FRANK	Well, if you're quite sure?
FIONA	(pushing the bottle gently to one side and picking up the newspaper) Yes, that's quite alright, darling.
FRANK	(with increasing irritation) Had a bit of a job getting that, actually. Couldn't remember the name you see. Had this girl in the shop opening all the bottles, letting me have a sniff. Putting it all over herself, letting me have a sniff, you see. Well, I felt a bit of a fool in the end. Standing there in the middle of this big shop, sniffing away for dear life. Naturally, you see, people were starting to stare. Stare at me sniffing. They must have thought I had some sort of fetish, or something. (He stamps out U.L.)
FIONA	(after him) Thank you, darling. It was a lovely thought. Very sweet.
	(TERESA jumps up and crosses D.S. of sofa to table R. and sits at U.S. end and sorts out paper cuttings.)
BOB	As a matter of fact –
TERESA	What?
BOB	Do you know who I was out with last night?
TERESA	Who?

BOB	William.
TERESA	William who?
BOB	William Featherstone –
TERESA	William Featherstone? Oh him. Yes. Works in your office, doesn't he?
BOB	No. Well, same firm but different department.
TERESA	Oh, I see.
BOB	Yes, I was out with him.
TERESA	What doing?
BOB	Oh, you know. Drinking. Talking.
TERESA	I didn't know he was a friend of yours?
BOB	Well, no he's not really. We have a chat, now and again.
TERESA	Oh. I've only met him once, haven't I? Wasn't he at that dreadful office dance?
BOB	That's right.
TERESA	With his wife – what's her name?
BOB	Mary.
TERESA	That's it. I seem to remember they were awfully boring, weren't they? What did you want to ask him out for?
BOB	He asked me really –
TERESA	(rising and crossing to L. of BOB) Shouldn't have thought you and he had much in common.
BOB	Well – we talked shop – mostly.
TERESA	Till two in the morning?
BOB	That and – other things.
TERESA	Wish you'd talk to me till two in the morning, and other things – What else did you talk about, then?
BOB	Um – Oh –
TERESA	(snatching the paper from BOB) I think you're making all this up. I can't believe you were out with him all that time –

BOB	Well, where else do you think I was, then?
TERESA	(throwing the paper at BOB and crossing to sit U.S. of table R.) I dread to think.
FRANK	(off) Darling! Crisis! We're out of bathroom stationery.
FIONA	(with an enormous sigh, rising) Oh dear. (She calls.) Just a minute. (She goes out U.L.)
BOB	No. If you must know – William's – a bit – upset –
TERESA	Why?
BOB	Well, it's very complicated – but – he thinks his wife is having an affair –
TERESA	Mary?
BOB	That's what he thinks.
TERESA	I should think that's unlikely. Looking at Mary.
BOB	Oh, I don't know, though –
TERESA	She didn't look the sort to do that. Very twitchy. Can't see anyone running after her –
BOB	She's not bad looking, at all –
TERESA	Oh –
BOB	Quite attractive, in fact – to a man.
TERESA	Really?
BOB	Not at all bad.
TERESA	Do you fancy her?
BOB	Well, not personally, no. But I know a lot of people who do.
TERESA	Who's she going off with, then?
BOB	William doesn't know. It's all very secret, you mustn't say anything. He was very cut up about it, though.
TERESA	Poor William. Oh dear. They haven't got any children, have they?
BOB	No. He's a great planner is William.

TERESA	Oh, well then. Did you advise him?
BOB	I told him it would probably blow over.
TERESA	(rising and crossing to L. of BOB)　　Yes, that's what you usually do.
BOB	What else could I say?
TERESA	Well, sometimes things don't. Unless you do something positive. Sometimes you really have to do something. (She paces and gestures L. and R.)　　You can't just say – oh, Benjamin's ill, it'll blow over – the house is on fire, it'll blow over. Sometimes it isn't enough just to sit back.
BOB	And what was I supposed to have done then?
TERESA	He wanted advice. He came to you – God knows why – for advice.
BOB	You can't advise in those sort of circumstances.
TERESA	Of course you could.　　(She crosses to L. of BOB and leans over him.)　　If you'd been a trained marriage guidance councillor you could have done. I mean, you could have told him at least to talk to her. It may be that there's all sorts of things, that with a talk they could clear the whole thing up.
	(FIONA enters U.L. and goes to phone.)
BOB	How do you reckon Benjamin's getting on out there on his own?
TERESA	Oh, I'd forgotten him.　　(She hurries out L.)　　I bet he's eating the soap flakes again –
	(BOB smartens himself up; preparing to leave. FIONA finishes dialling. BOB's phone rings. He answers it.)
BOB	Hallo.
	(FRANK enters U.L. and crosses D.S. to L. of FIONA.)
FIONA	Just a rinse and set would be lovely ...
FRANK	Darling – Do you know where the –
FIONA	(holding hand over receiver)　　Darling, I wonder if you'd be a poppet and get the car out into the drive for me?

I always ladder myself squeezing into that garage.

FRANK   Well, I was just looking for the screwdriver.

FIONA   Bless you, darling. Hallo, yes, yes . . . .

               (FRANK crosses U.S. and exits U.L.)

BOB   Has he gone?

FIONA   (as FRANK goes)   Just about. Yes. Can you talk?

BOB   Yes. Just for a second though. I'm just off to work.

FIONA   No, well, I've got to be quick. Listen, do you know
               what last night was?

BOB   Absolutely marvellous.

FIONA   It was my bloody wedding anniversary.

BOB   Oh, really? Congratulations.

FIONA   Oh, yes, it's a scream. I feel terrible about it.

               (TERESA enters from the kitchen, suddenly.)

TERESA   Bob!

BOB   Yes?

FIONA   What?

TERESA   Do you know what that child has done with an entire jar of
               honey –

BOB   (into phone)   Yes, well listen old man, I suggest your
               best bet is to divide the whole figure by two thirds . . .

FIONA   Is she there?

BOB   (cheerfully)   Yes.

TERESA   Where's the dishcloth?

BOB   (picking it up off the phone table and tossing it to her)
               Here.

TERESA   (going)   You would not believe what that child of
               yours has done with an entire jar of honey.   (She goes
               out in to the kitchen.)

BOB   I'm sorry, you were saying – ?

FIONA	Listen, the point is Frank's getting rather curious as to where I was.
BOB	That's funny. Same here.
FIONA	What do I tell him?
BOB	You were with a friend.
FIONA	No. He knows practically everyone, it's too risky ...
BOB	Look, I've got to go in a minute ...
FIONA	You haven't told me what I'm going to say ...
BOB	I don't know.
FIONA	What did you tell Terry, then?
BOB	That I ran into someone.
FIONA	Who?
BOB	William Featherstone.
FIONA	Who on earth is William Featherstone?
BOB	He works in the Accounts Department at the office. Anyway, he's married to Mary Featherstone ...
FIONA	Oh, Lord, I remember them. What on earth made you think of them ...
BOB	They're safe, obscure ... They're the first names that came into my head anyway ...
FIONA	Go on. What?
BOB	Their marriage is breaking up. Third party ...
FIONA	Really, I didn't know.
BOB	No, not really. That's just the story. But since it's all very hush hush nobody's to say a word ...
TERESA	(off) Bob – Bob – come and look at this –
BOB	Coming! Look I must go ... Say what you like ...
FIONA	But what about ... ?
	(BOB puts down phone.)
TERESA	(off) Bob –

(BOB crosses D.L. and exits kitchen L.)

FIONA   Bob –

BOB   (going off)   What?

(FRANK enters U.L.)

FRANK   What?

FIONA   Oh, have you brought the car out?

FRANK   (coming down steps and crossing behind settee)   It's already in the drive. You didn't put it away last night.

FIONA   Oh. How silly of me.

FRANK   No. Couple of wheels in the flower bed, actually.

FIONA   (crossing to FRANK)   You must go –

FRANK   Yes. I was – Have you seen that screwdriver –

FIONA   Screwdriver?

FRANK   Screwdriver. You know for screwing things. I've got to take the end off that toothbrush to get at the batteries. (He crosses U.L. and searches in drinks cabinet.)

FIONA   You don't want to do that now –

FRANK   Might as well do it now as later – Don't want to spend the evening sitting in the bathroom with a screwdriver. Have you put it anywhere?

FIONA   (crossing to R. of FRANK and guiding him towards kitchen R.)   Have you tried the toolbox.

FRANK   Toolbox?

FIONA   In the scullery.

FRANK   Oh, that toolbox. In there is it? Wondered where that had got to. Looking for a hammer only the other day. (He goes out R.)

(FIONA leans against door joint L. of kitchen door.)

FIONA   (calling)   You'll have to hurry.

(BOB enters from kitchen L. with one shoe off and clutching a blue folder and crosses U.S. of sofa and D.S.

of FIONA to wastepaper basket D.R.   FIONA steps D.S. to R. of sofa.)

TERESA	(off) Bob –
BOB	What is it?

(TERESA comes in L. and crosses U.S. of FIONA to L. of BOB.)

TERESA	Bob – Don't you think I'm right, that if William and Mary could just get together –
BOB	(crossing D.S. of sofa searching with TERESA following) Look, Terry, I'm late. Forget all about William and Mary and find my shoe –
TERESA	I haven't had it –
BOB	There's nothing we can do about it, it's supposed to be a dead secret, anyway –

(BOB crosses U.S. to C. and TERESA follows to his R.)

TERESA	What sort of shoe?
BOB	(pointing at his foot) The same as this one. Only pointing the other way –
TERESA	I don't know why you think I should have had it. (She walks round BOB and then goes out into kitchen L.)

(FIONA sits on R. arm of sofa.)

BOB	(yelling after her and crossing towards kitchen waving file) I think you might have had it for the same reason as you had this file of last year's estimated growth figures which I found in the breadbin – If you'd stop worrying a minute about other people and start organising this place a bit, I think you'd be making a very valuable contribution to world peace – (He crosses back to C.)
TERESA	It's alright, I've found it. Stop fussing. (She enters from kitchen L. and crosses to L. of BOB holding out a brown shoe and then notices that BOB is wearing a black shoe.) Oh –
BOB	Well, it might do as a novelty –
TERESA	I don't know where it is –

BOB   Never mind. Perhaps if I walk sideways no one will
               notice.   (He crosses D.R. and puts shoe into waste-
               paper basket and searches under table.)

               (TERESA crosses D.S. and searches under L. end of sofa.)

FRANK   (entering from R. with a box)   Not in here. No
               screwdriver in here.   (He leans over back of sofa to
               show FIONA shoe-box.)

               (TERESA crosses D.L. and searches round armchair.)

FIONA   I wouldn't imagine there would be, darling.

FRANK   You distinctly told me –

FIONA   Those are the shoe brushes.

FRANK   Shoe brushes. What are they doing in the toolbox?

FIONA   I'll show you.   (She rises and guides FRANK to kitchen
               door. They go out into kitchen.)

               (BOB crosses to D.L. and TERESA crosses to D.R. crossing
               C. BOB finds shoe in dolls' house R. of playpen.)

TERESA   Oh, there it is.   (She crosses to R. of BOB.)

BOB   (sitting in armchair D.L.)   How did it get in there,
               for crying out loud –

TERESA   Oh, I think I gave it to Benjy to play with last night –

BOB   Well, for heavens sake, why not buy him some toys? I
               mean why does he have to play with –   (As BOB pulls
               on shoe a strange sound comes from it. BOB puts his hand
               in and pulls out a toy squeaker.)   What's this?
               (He holds it up.)

TERESA   Oh, that's his moo-moo! He loves playing farms with
               your shoes –

BOB   (savagely)   Well, tell him to buy his own.   (He
               throws squeaker into playpen D.L.)

TERESA   Honestly, the way you talk about him, sometimes, terrifies
               me. You're supposed to be his father –

BOB   Terry.   (He rises and crosses to table D.R. and collects
               file.)   I'm late. I am very late. Now do me a favour.

During today, just go round very slowly and try and
straighten up this tip, will you?

(TERESA crosses to D.C. BOB crosses to R. of TERESA.)

TERESA   Oh, that's lovely. Here I am, stuck in this house day
                after day with that kid –

BOB   And here is five pounds. Five whole pounds. Now go
                mad. Go out to the nearest shop and try buying a little
                food. Not just jars of peanut butter – but food –
                (He crosses U.S. to door U.R. and grabs raincoat.)

TERESA   (following to step)   Oh go on, clear out –

BOB   (opening front door and turning in doorway)   And
                another thing, wash that child, will you? He's got
                enough food plastered round his face to feed a family of
                four.   (He goes out U.R. and slams door.)

                (TERESA crosses and puts money on dresser U.R. and then
                crosses D.R. and collects phone directory from under
                table.)

TERESA   That's right. Walk out, go on. You're no help, you're
                no help at all are you?

                (TERESA circles the room muttering and making ineffectual
                and rather violent tidying motions. She picks up the
                phone book, consults it, finds the number she wants, rips
                out the page, crosses to the phone and dials. FIONA
                enters R. and goes to the phone, dials, gets an engaged
                signal and irritatedly hangs up. She goes off to the hall
                U.L.)

TERESA   Hallo ... is that Mary Featherstone? Oh well, I don't
                know if you'll remember me, but my name is Teresa
                Phillips ...   Yes, that's right ... yes. Look, Mary, this
                may seem a bit out of the blue, but Bob and I were
                wondering if you and your husband would like to come
                over to dinner some night... Well, what about tonight?...
                Oh, are you? Well, what about tomorrow, then? You
                are? Super. Let's make it tomorrow ... Friday ...

                (FRANK enters R. using screwdriver on the toothbrush.)

                ... about eight. Yes. Yes. 'Bye.   (She hangs up

and goes into the kitchen L.)

FIONA   (entering from the hall with FRANK's hat, coat and umbrella)   Have, you done it?

FRANK   Not yet. One has to be careful with these things not to give oneself a shock. It's rather more sophisticated than I imagined – ah!   (The toothbrush collapses.)

FIONA   (who hasn't noticed)   Well done, darling.

FRANK   (rising with toothbrush and crossing to U.R. of chair) No, it appears to have come apart. Isn't that typical British workmanship? Came to pieces in my hands.

FIONA   (crossing to L. of FRANK)   Darling, you've unscrewed the wrong bit. The batteries go in there. You really are hopeless.   (Holding out his coat.)   Here we are.

FRANK   (struggling into coat)   Perfectly useless. The only people who understand these things are the Japanese and they're never here when you want them. Now then. (He takes hat and umbrella.)   Hat, umbrella, toothbrush.

FIONA   You'll have to hurry.

FRANK   Just want to drop this in at the garage. Get them to have a look at it. Something not right with it.

FIONA   Leave that now, darling. Have you got your briefcase?

FRANK   (peering at the breakfast table)   Yes, it's in the – er –   (He crosses D.S. and picks up perfume from his breakfast table.)   If you told me the name of your stuff, I could have this changed, you see –

FIONA   Now, do hurry, darling –

FRANK   Yes.   (He looks at his watch.)   Good Lord, yes – Where on earth is my – er –

FIONA   In the hall.   (She crosses U.S. onto steps U.L.)

FRANK   (crossing to coffee table and picking up TV Times) Very good programme on the television, last night, you know. You'd have liked it –

FIONA   I'll get your briefcase.   (She goes out U.L.)

FRANK   (crossing to armchair C. and calling after her)   It was about this man who – there were two of them to start with, but one had to drop out with a pulled muscle. Anyway, this other fellow tackled it on his own. Damn near brought it off too –

FIONA   (entering U.L. and handing FRANK his briefcase) Here you are –

(FRANK sits C. and puts TV Times into briefcase and hands FIONA toothbrush and screwdriver.)

FRANK   This – er – this – no, that's right. There were three of them to start with. One had the pulled muscle and the other one had – er – whatever happened to the other one? I know there was only one left in the end – Oh, he died. That's it. He died, which left only this one chap, you see –

(FRANK rises and crosses U.S. to doors U.L. FIONA follows to his L. and kisses his cheek.)

FIONA   Off you go. Off you go now. Bye bye.   (She hands him his briefcase.)

FRANK   Yes – bye, bye darling. Lovely to have seen you. (He goes out U.L.)

(FIONA leans on L. door. FRANK re-enters through R. door.)

Whatever happened to you last night. You didn't tell me, did you –

FIONA   (crossing D.S. and picking up perfume from FRANK's breakfast table)   Didn't I?

FRANK   No. I was a bit puzzled, because I thought I heard you say earlier that you were going to that meeting, but then this Mrs – er – thing rings up and says you haven't turned up.   (He crosses D.S. to L. of FIONA.)   Got a bit worried – Didn't break down, did you? No, you can't have done – Wheels in the flowerbed.

FIONA   (with a deep breath)   No, well, actually – I decided to skip that wretched meeting for once and hurry home. I was on my way, and then – who should I run into but Mary

Featherstone –

FRANK   Mary Featherstone? Who's Mary Featherstone?

FIONA   She's William Featherstone's wife, darling. Doesn't he
         work with you?

FRANK   William Feath – oh, yes, yes – he does, indeed. How
         odd. Didn't know you two were friendly. That's good.

FIONA   Well, we hardly – I mean hardly at all. Just one of
         those dreary office parties, that's the only time –

FRANK   Well, you certainly made a night of it, I must say –

         (FIONA crosses and sits R. end of sofa and indicates that
         FRANK should sit beside her. FRANK crosses and sits C.
         of sofa.)

FIONA   Yes, well, the point is – Now this is terribly secret,
         darling, you mustn't say a word to anyone –

FRANK   What is?

FIONA   Promise?

FRANK   Of course. What?

FIONA   Well, Mary is terribly upset.

FRANK   Why?

FIONA   I'm just telling you.

FRANK   I'm sorry, dear.

FIONA   Putting it all in the crudest possible terms – she's pretty
         sure that William has another woman.

FRANK   Another one?

FIONA   (as to a child)   An affair, darling. A love affair.

FRANK   Good Lord. Good Lord. Good heavens, Featherstone?

FIONA   Yes.

FRANK   Good grief. This is shattering –

FIONA   Yes, well Mary was very upset, of course. And for some
         reason she chose to pour it all out to me – but you mustn't
         say a word darling –

FRANK   No, quite. Well, I must say, I'm absolutely shattered by this –

FIONA   Yes. Of course, we hardly know them – but all the same –

FRANK   That's beside the point.   (He rises and crosses L.) Whether we know them or not's beside the point –

FIONA   Is it? Why?

FRANK   Ah, well. Something you didn't know, you see. Didn't tell you. Featherstone's due to join us.

FIONA   Us who?

FRANK   My department. All fixed. He's transferring from accounts and joining us –

FIONA   (blankly)   Oh, is he?

FRANK   That's the idea. Expanding you see. So he's due to join us. Key job.   (He crosses and sits in armchair C.) He's not going to be much good if he's got all this sort of carry on – Are you sure? He seems a very quiet sort of fellow. Not the sort of chap who'd dash off the rails. Is this wife of his sure of her facts?

FIONA   Well, I suppose she is, yes.   (She rises and crosses U.S.)   I suppose she could possibly be wrong –

FRANK   Mind you, if she's upset enough to talk to a near stranger till God knows when in the morning –

FIONA   (crossing to table L., putting down perfume and picking up tray)   Tell me, does Bob Phillips know about this appointment?

FRANK   Phillips, no. Why should he?

FIONA   Well, I thought, seeing as he's in your department – ?

FRANK   Oh, no, no, no. Can't announce these things prematurely you know.

         (FIONA crosses R. to U.S. of sofa and then exits into kitchen R.)

         Board decision.   (He sees the toothbrush on the table.) That's odd. I thought I had that with me. Darling, have we got two of these things? No, no, Phillips'll be told

	this morning. I'm announcing it. Told Featherstone a couple of days ago, put him out of his agony, but can't start leaking things like this – not until all the candidates have been notified –
FIONA	Yes, I see.
FRANK	(rising and crossing D.S. to D.C.) Good Lord, I say, this is going to be very embarrassing tonight, isn't it?
FIONA	What is?
FRANK	I mean I had no idea at the time –
FIONA	(entering from kitchen R. and crossing R. of sofa to R. of FRANK) What?
FRANK	That the Featherstones – Oh, now I know, I know, I know – Now I know. I know what it was I was thinking last night when you didn't get back. I remember thinking – good heavens I remember thinking, I mustn't forget. I remember thinking –
FIONA	Darling, what are you trying to say?
FRANK	I've invited the Featherstone's to dinner.
FIONA	Tonight?
FRANK	Yes.
FIONA	Oh, that's out of the question –
FRANK	You're not going out are you?
FIONA	Well, I may be –
FRANK	Well, can't you cancel it? Where are you going?
FIONA	– Um – nowhere, no. I'm not going out.
FRANK	Oh, that's fine. Fine. Sorry if I've caught you with your – er – guard down – lowered – but I'm sure you'll cope. Absolutely sure. Must dash – (He kisses FIONA and crosses U.S. onto steps.) See you – er – They'll be coming about eight, by the way – Do I need a coat?
FIONA	You've got one on.

FRANK	Yes, right. Dinner at eight – did I tell you? (He goes out.)
FIONA	(dully) Cheer-o.

(FRANK exits U.L. FIONA crosses U.S. and looks at doors and then crosses D.S. to phone. TERESA enters from kitchen L. and crosses to front door U.R. with boxes. FIONA dials and then drops toothbrush into wastepaper basket. As phone rings TERESA crosses to table R. drops boxes on table and crosses and answers phone. FRANK enters U.L. and crosses to R. of FIONA.)

FRANK	Ah! (He points somewhat accusingly at FIONA.)
FIONA	(hiding phone) What's that, darling?
FRANK	Toothbrush.
FIONA	Mmm?
FRANK	Forgot the toothbrush, didn't I? Where's it gone?
FIONA	There. (She points at waste paper basket.) I'm afraid I threw it away.
FRANK	(holding up basket and peering in) Ah! (He wanders to the door still with basket.) Caught you this time.
TERESA	(answering the phone) Hallo ....
FRANK	Now then, where's the – er –
FIONA	What's the matter, darling?
TERESA	Hallo?

(FRANK crosses to drinks cabinet U.L. and searches in drawer. FIONA hides phone under cushion and crosses to L. of FRANK.)

FRANK	Can't seem to – see it – anywhere –
FIONA	What?

(FRANK doesn't reply but wanders round peering under furniture, etc.)

TERESA	Hallo, who is that?

(FRANK exits into kitchen R. and FIONA follows.)

FIONA   What are you looking for?

FRANK   The – thingummyjig.   (He gestures vaguely.)

(They search.)

TERESA   Hallo. Look – if you're one of those sort of callers – You'd better hang up at once.

FRANK   You haven't thrown that away, too, have you?

FIONA   Thrown what away?

TERESA   I'm warning you, my husband is very strong. He's a wrestler. He has a very bad temper. And we also have dogs. Enormous dogs –   (She pauses to see what effect this has had.)

(FRANK enters from the kitchen R. and goes to armchair C.)

FIONA   Darling, what are we looking for?

(FRANK picks up cushion and finds receiver.)

FRANK   (lifting receiver absently to see if it's under there) Screwdriver.

TERESA   Uh? AND YOU!

(FRANK puts receiver down and crosses to table L. and sees screwdriver on coffee table. TERESA puts down phone and crosses U.S.)

FRANK   Ah! It's alright, darling, I've got it. Don't panic. Got it.

(FIONA enters from kitchen R. FRANK crosses to U.C.)

FIONA   Good darling. Bye bye now.

FRANK   Dinner at eight – did I tell you? Bye.   (He exits U.L.)

FIONA   (closing doors)   Dinner at eight. Mmm.

TERESA   Mmm.

(FIONA and TERESA cross D.S. to telephone tables and pick up pads and pencils.)

FIONA	(thoughtfully) Avocado –
TERESA	Packet of chicken noodle soup.
FIONA	Courgettes.
TERESA	Sprouts.
FIONA	Sour cream.
TERESA	Spuds.
FIONA	Pork.
TERESA	Chops.
FIONA	Marron glacé.
TERESA	Treacle pud.
FIONA	Kirsch –
TERESA	(as an afterthought) Booze!

CURTAIN

Scene Two

The set is the same as in Act I, Scene One except both dining tables have been moved to U.L. The FOSTER's table is parallel to the stage edge with the PHILLIPS' slightly higher table placed across it at right angles to form a 'T' shape with the top of the 'T' facing D.S. The FOSTER's C. armchair is placed U.R.   U.L. of tables is the FOSTER's trolley. The FOSTER's two dining chairs are at the narrow end of their table and the PHILLIPS' two dining chairs are at the narrow ends of their table. There are two swivel chairs in the angles of the 'T'. The three settee seats now all match the FOSTER's decor.

Evening.

FIONA enters from kitchen R. with tray of glasses and napkins. TERESA enters from kitchen L. with tumblers and packet of napkins. They cross D.S.

of dining table. FIONA crosses to U.L. of dining table and puts tray on
trolley. TERESA crosses to U.R. of her table, puts down glasses etc. and
then crosses U.S. and switches on light U.R. and crosses back to table.
FIONA polishes glasses and puts one at each place and then folds and lays
napkins. TERESA places tumblers crosses U.S. to Welsh dresser and empties
pencils out of glass and crosses back to table. TERESA attempts to fold paper
napkins, fails and pushes a napkin into each soup bowl. They end up
surveying table. FIONA U.R. of her table, TERESA U.L. of hers.

	(FIONA's door slams, off. She looks up. TERESA's door slams, off. She looks up.)
FRANK	(off) Darling –
BOB	(off) Terry –
FIONA	In here, dear.
TERESA	Hallo.
	(FRANK enters U.L. crosses and kisses FIONA on cheek, hands her wet newspaper. BOB enters U.R. and crosses D.S. TERESA extends arms for embrace. BOB passes her and crosses and sits in armchair D.L.)
FRANK	Hallo, darling.
FIONA	(without looking up) Hallo.
BOB	Hi!
TERESA	'Llo.
FRANK	Filthy night, you know. Absolutely filthy.
FIONA	Pour me a drink, darling, will you? I'm dying for one.
FRANK	(going to do so) Um.
	(TERESA crosses to U.S. of BOB and puts arms round his neck. BOB reads paper.)
TERESA	Want some tea?
BOB	In a minute.
FIONA	(crossing and putting paper on trolley and moving trolley to D.L. of her table) You did say eight o'clock, didn't you?

FRANK   – Er, more or less, I think.

(FIONA crosses to window, draws curtains and then crosses to U.S. of table and switches on light L. of main door. She crosses and sits R. end of sofa.)

FIONA   I mean if they arrive any earlier I'm just not going to be ready, that's all.

TERESA   I'll put the kettle on.   (She exits into kitchen L.)

BOB   Fine. Thank God it's Friday, that's all I can say.

FRANK   (pouring sherry at the sideboard)   By George, there's been a downpour tonight. Absolutely pouring down.

FIONA   I know. And that back drain's flooding again, as a result.

FRANK   Is it? Is it? Oh well, I'll get out there and have a poke around with a stick later on. I'll drag the old wellies out. Have a prod.

FIONA   If you don't mind my saying so, I don't think your prods are awfully effective, darling. It was nearly up to the window sill last time I looked.

FRANK   (crossing D.S., handing FIONA sherry and sitting C. of sofa)   Here we are.

FIONA   Thank you, darling.   (She drinks.)   Mmmm. Lovely. You know, I don't know how I've got through today, I really don't. I must just ask you one thing, darling. If you must spring these surprise dinner parties on me, please don't do it on a Thursday again. It's one of my busiest days as it is.

FRANK   Well, you seem pretty busy most days to me. What's so special about Thursday?

FIONA   Well, for one thing. The Thursday Guild Meeting.

FRANK   Oh yes, of course. I forgot that was on Thursdays, yes.

FIONA   Anyway, I hope these people are going to be worth it.

FRANK   Oh, I should think so. He's a – he's a bright enough little fellow. Of course you know her, don't you?

FIONA   Do I? Only very slightly. And remember, darling, we're
             not going to mention anything about that, are we?

FRANK   Mmmm?

FIONA   About William and – er –

FRANK   Oh. Oh, good Lord, no. I'd strongly advise you not to
             mention it –

FIONA   Fine. No confrontations, then?

FRANK   No need.

FIONA   Just a jolly evening. How splendid. Cheers.

FRANK   Cheers.
             (They sit drinking.)

BOB   (rising and crossing to D.S. of his dining table)   Terry!

TERESA   (off)   What?

BOB   What's all this in aid of?

TERESA   (off)   Oh. I'll tell you. In a second.

BOB   (glaring at the table)   If you've asked your mother
             round –

FRANK   No, he's quite a decent sort, old Featherstone. Quite a
             decent sort. He has some extraordinary hobby in his spare
             time. Can't remember what it is. Wears boots for it.
             Keeps them on top of his filing cabinet –

BOB   (crossing R. of table and U.S. to kitchen door L)
             Terry. Who is coming?

TERESA   (off)   Wait.

FRANK   Large boots. Don't know what he gets up to in them,
             though. It isn't mountaineering. I'll tell you that much.
             (TERESA enters from kitchen L. to L. of BOB. FRANK
             rises and crosses U.S. to drinks cabinet.)

TERESA   (handing BOB a mug of tea)   Here we are. It is
             sugared.

BOB   And who have you invited for dinner tonight?

(TERESA crosses to Welsh dresser for candle and crosses to U.R. of her table and puts candle C. of table.)

TERESA	I wish you wouldn't shout. I've only just this minute got Benjamin off to sleep.
BOB	(quietly, crossing to U.L. of his table) I am asking you – who?
FRANK	And it wasn't rock-climbing, either –
TERESA	Well – the Featherstones, actually. (She crosses U.S. of BOB and exits into kitchen L.)
BOB	(after a pause) I see – (He sits U.S. of table.)
FRANK	(crossing D.S. to L. of sofa) I'll tell you something else though. Whatever he gets up to in these boots of his, he doesn't take his wife. I know that. Goes off on his own. Which either means that it's dangerous. Or else – or else it's tied up with this other business. That's a point – (He ponders, then crosses U.S. to drinks cabinet.)

(TERESA enters from kitchen L. and crosses to L. of table and picks up packet of napkins.)

BOB	And what exactly do you intend to do? Sort out their marriage over dinner?
TERESA	Of course not.
BOB	Well?
TERESA	If friends need help –
BOB	They will ask for it. Exactly. When did you decide to ask them round here?
TERESA	Yesterday morning. After you'd told me.
BOB	I see. And now we have to sit through a whole evening of them, do we? We have to put up with the most excruciating evening, just because you have nothing better to do with your time.
TERESA	I have plenty of other –
BOB	Then mind your own business.
TERESA	If you had a scrap of sensitivity –
BOB	I'm sensitive enough to know when people want to be left

alone.

TERESA	Well. It's too late now, isn't it. They're coming. (She exits into kitchen L.)
FRANK	(crossing D.S. to U.L. of sofa) Do you think this is a possibility? He uses those boots of his to tramp off and see this other woman of his. Perhaps she lives on a marsh, or something. Which would explain why he keeps them in the office. He doesn't want his wife to see them. You see?
FIONA	(rising and crossing to U.R. of sofa) Darling. I do wish you'd look at that drain, before too long. And I must get ready. I seem to remember they were awfully sombre people. I do hope they won't be too impossible.
FRANK	Good Lord, no. What did you think of my theory about those boots of his, by the way?
FIONA	Well, I suppose it's feasible, darling. But I do think it's a trifle oblique – (She starts to go.)
FRANK	Yes, I'd better go and look out that stick for the drain. You haven't moved it, I hope.
	(FIONA crosses to kitchen doorway R. FRANK starts to follow, but she indicates that he go the other way.)
FIONA	No, it's round the back, behind the garage, I think. I should go out the front door and round that way. It's ankle deep in the yard. (She exits into kitchen R.)
FRANK	(crossing to double doors) Yes. Right. Well, throw me a line if I – oh, never mind. (He exits U.L.)
	(TERESA enters from kitchen L. switches on light L. of kitchen door, and then crosses to window R.)
BOB	(rising) Well, if I'm expected to spend an evening with those two, I'm entitled to a drink.
TERESA	I've bought some.
BOB	Where?
TERESA	(drawing curtains R. and pointing to a bottle of white wine on the table) There.

BOB   (studying the bottle disgustedly) Oh my God –

TERESA   (alarmed) It's not South African, is it?

BOB   (crossing U.S. to front door U.R.) I'm going out now –

TERESA   (crossing to L. of BOB) You can't!

BOB   I can!

TERESA   How long for?

BOB   A bit – (He goes out U.R.)

TERESA   Bob –

BOB   (shouting back) It depends –

TERESA   Bob!

(TERESA stands for a moment, undecided. Then, impetuously she snatches a coat from the pegs near U.R. door, hurries to the other door L. and listens a moment for Benjamin. Seemingly all is well for after a second she dashes out of the front door in pursuit of BOB. She pulls the door to but does not latch it. The stage is empty for a second. Silence. Both doorbells ring. A pause. They ring again. WILLIAM peers round double doors U.L. MARY peers around front door U.R. A few moments then WILLIAM and MARY enter, both in their thirties. He wears a soaking wet mac and enters through FIONA's front door. She, although in a coat, is bone dry. She enters through TERESA's door.)

WILLIAM   (calling) Hallo –

MARY   (calling) Hallo –

(WILLIAM and MARY move cautiously and cross D.S., meeting U.C. They look at each other.)

WILLIAM   Nobody here.

MARY   Funny.

WILLIAM   Very odd.

MARY   (anxiously) We're not early are we?

WILLIAM   Of course we're not.

MARY	(calling off one way) Hallo!
WILLIAM	No, don't do that. Don't do that.
MARY	Let them know we're here.
WILLIAM	Well, we can just wait quietly. Don't have to shout about. They'll be here when they're ready, I expect –
MARY	Table's laid.
WILLIAM	Oh yes?
MARY	(nervously laughing) We're expected, anyway –
WILLIAM	Yes, well we would be.
MARY	(wandering R. and back to R. of WILLIAM, nibbling her nails) Oh – I feel awful just, walking into their house. I –
WILLIAM	Now don't start to get nervous. There's nothing at all to get nervous about. Just keep calm. (He takes her hand from her mouth and smacks it like he would a child's.) Sit down if you want to.
MARY	No, I won't sit down – I –
WILLIAM	Did you take your tablets?
MARY	Yes –
	(WILLIAM puts arm round MARY and then crosses L. and D.S., L. of FIONA's table to D.L. of FIONA's table.)
WILLIAM	Good. Now you just have to be natural. No need to put on any act. No need at all. Just be yourself –
MARY	Yes. It's just I – never – seem to be able to say anything.
WILLIAM	You don't have to if you don't want to. Nobody's asking you to say anything unless you feel you want to –
MARY	But if I don't I feel so – so –
	(FIONA enters from kitchen R.)
FIONA	Darling I –
	(MARY hides behind WILLIAM. WILLIAM steps forward. FIONA crosses D.S. to R. of WILLIAM.)

	Oh, Good Lord. You're here. Hallo.
WILLIAM	Hallo. Sorry to surprise you, but we rang a couple of times – didn't get a reply – and the door was off the latch, so we –
FIONA	Oh, well. Good heavens, yes, very sensible of you. Frank must have left it open. He's having a go at our drains – Good heavens, let me take your coat. You're soaked.
WILLIAM	Quite a downpour.
FIONA	Yes. What a downpour.

(WILLIAM turns to take his coat off. FIONA crosses D.S. of WILLIAM to R. of MARY, who backs away.)

And how are you, Mary?

MARY	(inaudible) Oh. Fine, thank you.
FIONA	Mmmm?
WILLIAM	She's had a bit of a cold, haven't you Mary, but I think she's over it now.
FIONA	Oh, I'm sorry to hear that. (She takes WILLIAM's coat.) I'll just pop that in the hall, let it dry out – Then we can all have a sherry. (She crosses U.S. L. of table and exits U.L.
WILLIAM	(crossing U.S., R. of table holding out hat) Very charming, isn't she. Very charming woman.
MARY	(in an undertone crossing to U.L. of table) I don't like sherry.
WILLIAM	(crossing U.S. of sofa) Well, just ask for a small glass, then.
MARY	But it gives me terrible indigestion.
WILLIAM	(crossing to R. of sofa) Well, say you'd like a cream sherry. You liked the cream sherry we had at Bertha's at Christmas.
MARY	No, I didn't. Bertha just kept giving it to me. I didn't like it at all. Shall I ask if I can have a tonic water?

WILLIAM   You can't ask her for a tonic water. People don't drink tonic water. Not for an hors d'oeuvres –

MARY   (desperately)   Well, what shall I say?

(FIONA enters U.L. and crosses to drinks cabinet. WILLIAM hides his hat under sofa cushion R.)

FIONA   I've put it just by the radiator. Should be dry in no time. Now then what are we all having? Mary?

MARY   Um –

FIONA   What would you like?

MARY   Er –

FIONA   Sherry?

MARY   Well I –

FIONA   Medium? Or would you prefer dry?

MARY   Thank you very much.

FIONA   Dry. William?

WILLIAM   Same again, please.

FIONA   Three dry. Jolly good.   (She pours sherry.)

WILLIAM   Very nice room.

FIONA   Thank you.

WILLIAM   Very nice indeed. Very tasteful.

FIONA   Here we are, Mary –   (She crosses to MARY with sherry.)

(MARY goes to take sherry and finds she is wearing her gloves, she pulls it off and takes sherry. FIONA crosses back to drinks cabinet and takes two sherries and crosses D.S. L. of sofa and hands WILLIAM sherry. MARY crosses D.S. L. of table to R. of BOB's armchair.)

FIONA   Well, I suppose we drink to your new job William.

WILLIAM   Well, thank you.

FIONA   Cheers, then.

WILLIAM   Good health.

(They drink. MARY coughs.)

FIONA   Oh, dear. Alright?

MARY   Thank you. Alright –   (She hiccups.)

FIONA   Yes, Frank's absolutely delighted you're joining the department. He speaks awfully highly of you. Awfully highly.

WILLIAM   Pleased to hear it.

FIONA   You're absolutely wizard with figures apparently?

WILLIAM   Yes, well I've always been interested in them.

        (MARY hiccups.)

        Seemed to come naturally –

FIONA   In that case, I think you're awfully clever. I'm afraid I'm hopeless. I can't even add up the shopping list. Then I'm afraid that's just women, isn't it?

        (MARY hiccups.)

WILLIAM   Yes, I'm afraid you're right, there. I have to keep a firm eye on Mary's accounts, don't I Mary?

FIONA   Lucky you, Mary.

MARY   (smiling)   Yes.   (She hiccups and attempts to stifle them.)

        (A silence.)

FIONA   And what have you both been up to? Anything exciting?

WILLIAM   No, no.

FIONA   Oh. Well, it's been pretty dull all round for everyone, hasn't it?   (Pause.)   I mean, I always think these things go in phases, don't they. You have an exciting bit of the year. And then all of a sudden you get a dull bit of the year.   (Pause.)   I don't know why that should be, at all, do you? But I've always found that, for some reason.   (Pause.)   Must be to do with the time of year I suppose. In the summer you can always get out, can't you? But then when you come to winter, on a day like today, and you can't do anything really.

You're just stuck indoors all day. Wishing you could get out. Only you can't. You have to sit indoors, waiting till the dreary old weather gets brighter again.
(Pause.)   Look, I think I really ought to dash out and drag Frank in.   (She crosses U.S., R. of table and puts glass on drinks cabinet.)   Not fair for him to miss all the fun, is it?   (She exits U.L.)

(WILLIAM and MARY cross U.S. WILLIAM to D.R. of steps and MARY to U.L. of table.)

MARY   She's very elegant, isn't she?

WILLIAM   Oh, well. She's used to this sort of thing.

(MARY puts glass on table.)

(crossing to R. of MARY)   Mr Foster must give dozens of these sort of informal dinner parties. She'll be used to entertaining people –

MARY   I don't think I could ever –   (She starts to nibble her nails again.)

WILLIAM   Oh, yes you will. Yes you will. You'll see.   (He smacks MARY's hand.)   We'll have to start doing this sort of thing soon, you know.

MARY   Oh, I hope we don't –   (She crosses towards window L.)

WILLIAM   (crossing U.S. to drinks cabinet and putting down glass) Well, people will expect it, you see. You can't just accept entertainment and not give it, can you. No need to worry. You'll soon find yourself enjoying these sort of things as much as she does, you'll see.

(TERESA's doorbell rings.)

MARY   (after a nervous pause)   What was that?

WILLIAM   The bell.

(The bell rings again.)

MARY   Who is it?

WILLIAM   Somebody wanting to get in.

MARY   Who?

WILLIAM	I don't know. Go and have a look.
MARY	Do you think I should?
WILLIAM	Go on.

(They stand either side of the door. MARY opens it gingerly. TERESA is revealed.)

TERESA	Hallo.
WILLIAM	Hallo Terry.
MARY	Hallo.
TERESA	(awkwardly) You're here. This is very unusual – the guests letting the hostess in.
WILLIAM	Very unusual.
MARY	That's alright.
WILLIAM	We rang the bell. But we thought you must have all died.
TERESA	No – actually – Bob's out – at the moment. He's just popped out. And I've been out, too, getting some air – Forgot my key. Will you excuse me? I must just see to Benjamin. (She moves to the kitchen door.)
MARY	How is he?
TERESA	Oh. Big. Fat. Spoilt.
MARY	(dismayed) Ah.
TERESA	No, actually he's super, but we don't tell him that or he'll get conceited, like his father. (She goes out to the bedroom.)
WILLIAM	Are you sure you got the telephone message right?
MARY	How do you mean?
WILLIAM	She doesn't exactly look ready to entertain.
MARY	Yes, Friday night. I remember. She wanted us to come last night only we couldn't because we had to go to the Foster's.
TERESA	(re-entering holding a wet nappy) Sorry. (To MARY.) Take your coat, shall I?

MARY

Thank you.   (She fumbles out of her coat.)

(TERESA, needing two hands to help her, hands WILLIAM the wet nappy. He takes it inadvertently. MARY removes her coat revealing a fairly awful dress. TERESA takes the coat and moves up to the door U.R. to hang it up. WILLIAM notices that MARY is still wearing her cardigan.)

WILLIAM

(urgently)   Cardigan!

MARY

What?

WILLIAM

Take off your cardigan.

(MARY whips it off and tucks it under her arm to conceal it. TERESA rejoins them having taken a fresh nappy from a pile by the door.)

TERESA

(noticing MARY's dress for the first time)   Oh. That's lovely –   (She sees she has left WILLIAM holding the nappy.)   Oh, sorry.   (She takes the nappy from WILLIAM and goes off into the kitchen.)

WILLIAM

(taking the cardigan from MARY and going to hang it up) I think I'd better wash my –

(TERESA has gone. He wipes his hands on his handkerchief.)

TERESA

(off)   Well, at least the weather's better than last night. Wasn't it terrible?

MARY

Yes, we were caught in it.

TERESA

Were you?   (She re-enters.)   Oh yes, how did that go?

WILLIAM

What's that?

TERESA

Your dinner with the big man. How did it go?

WILLIAM

Very pleasant. Very pleasant indeed.

TERESA

Yes, isn't Frank the sweetest old thing?

MARY

Oh, yes, I thought Mr Foster was very nice indeed –

TERESA

And how was the fabulous Fiona?

WILLIAM

Charming. I found her very charming indeed.

TERESA	Yes, she's certainly that. What did you think, Mary? Had you met her before?
MARY	Only once. At the party. I thought she was quite – nice.
TERESA	Yes. I think she gets on better with the men. I'm sorry. I think she's a bitch. (She crosses U.S. to kitchen doorway.)
WILLIAM	Oh, come now –
	(MARY crosses to R. of TERESA. WILLIAM crosses to her L.)
MARY	Can I have a peep at Benjamin later on?
TERESA	Yes, can you wait until he's gone off properly? Otherwise he'll be up all through dinner. I know him.
MARY	Alright.
TERESA	Would you excuse me a minute? I must just finish seeing to him. Sit down. Make yourselves comfy. (She exits into kitchen L.)
	(WILLIAM and MARY turn and face D.S. MARY crosses D.S. and sits in armchair D.L. WILLIAM crosses D.S. and wanders R. and L.)
WILLIAM	Sit, sit, sit. They could really make this room into something, if they put their minds to it.
MARY	I think Terry's looking awfully tired –
WILLIAM	Get it all repapered, lick of paint – make a proper difference that would –
MARY	I wonder where Bob's gone?
WILLIAM	Gone out, didn't she say?
MARY	That's what she said. I wonder why she invited us round?
WILLIAM	For a meal.
MARY	Never has before. We hardly know her really –
WILLIAM	(crossing to R. of MARY) I shall be working at the next desk to him, now.
MARY	It wasn't him who invited us, it was her.

MARY   Only once. At the party. I thought she was quite – nice.

TERESA   Yes. I think she gets on better with the men. I'm sorry.
              I think she's a bitch.   (She crosses U.S. to kitchen
              doorway.)

WILLIAM   Oh, come now –

              (MARY crosses to R. of TERESA. WILLIAM crosses to her
              L.)

MARY   Can I have a peep at Benjamin later on?

TERESA   Yes, can you wait until he's gone off properly? Otherwise
              he'll be up all through dinner. I know him.

MARY   Alright.

TERESA   Would you excuse me a minute? I must just finish seeing
              to him. Sit down. Make yourselves comfy.   (She
              exits into kitchen L.)

              (WILLIAM and MARY turn and face D.S. MARY crosses
              D.S. and sits in armchair D.L. WILLIAM crosses D.S. and
              wanders R. and L.)

WILLIAM   Sit, sit, sit. They could really make this room into
              something, if they put their minds to it.

MARY   I think Terry's looking awfully tired –

WILLIAM   Get it all repapered, lick of paint – make a proper
              difference that would –

MARY   I wonder where Bob's gone?

WILLIAM   Gone out, didn't she say?

MARY   That's what she said. I wonder why she invited us round?

WILLIAM   For a meal.

MARY   Never has before. We hardly know her really –

WILLIAM   (crossing to R. of MARY)   I shall be working at the
              next desk to him, now.

MARY   It wasn't him who invited us, it was her.

WILLIAM   I don't know what you're going on about, I'm sure.
                 (He crosses U.S., picks up glass from FIONA's drinks
                 cabinet and crosses to D.S. of steps. He is pacing up
                 and down, jigging about - he whistles to himself.)

                 (MARY rises, crosses U.S., picks up glass from table and
                 crosses to L. of WILLIAM.)

MARY   What's the matter?

WILLIAM   Matter?

MARY   Why are you - ?

WILLIAM   Nothing. Nothing at all.   (He paces a bit more.)
                 Just wondering where the - whereabouts their - that's all.

MARY   Upstairs?

WILLIAM   Probably. And downstairs, I wouldn't be surprised.

MARY   (impressed)   Two?

WILLIAM   In a house like this - knowing Mr Foster - almost bound to.

                 (FRANK enters from kitchen R., pauses and turns in
                 doorway.)

FRANK   Ah! Hallo there - darling, I thought you said Pinky and
                 Perky had arrived -

                 (WILLIAM breaks D.S. FRANK crosses D.S., R. of sofa.
                 WILLIAM crosses D.S., L. of sofa and MARY follows to L.
                 of WILLIAM.)

WILLIAM   Oh, hallo, Mr Foster. Have you met my wife, Mary -
                 Mr Foster.

MARY   How do you do?

FRANK   Yes, of course we've met. One of those - er do's. Office
                 do's.

MARY   Fancy remembering.

FRANK   Ah, well now. That's me you see. Always remember the -
                 er good looking women never their bloomin' husbands -

                 (WILLIAM and MARY laugh politely.)

                 Matter of fact. Let you into a secret. Everyone thinks

that I promoted your husband because he's the best man at his job. But that's not the real reason.

(MARY hides behind WILLIAM.)

After his lovely wife, actually.   (He crosses D.S. of WILLIAM and MARY and then U.S., L. of sofa to drinks cabinet.)

(WILLIAM pushes MARY U.S. and follows to her R.)

Both drinking are you? Think I'll join you. Been out in all this, poking about in the drains, for my sins. Have to excuse my socks - no shoes. Point is, changed into my boots -   (With a sudden sharp, significant look at WILLIAM.)   - Boots, did my bit with the stick out there, got back in here, someone'd pinched my shoes -

WILLIAM	Stolen them?
FRANK	Well, probably not stolen. More - moved them, perhaps.
MARY	I'm always losing things.
FRANK	Are you? (He crosses to L., of MARY.) Same as me.
WILLIAM	I'm always having to go round finding things for her.
FRANK	So's my wife. Gets absolutely hopping mad. Fill you up, can I?
WILLIAM	Thank you.
FRANK	Mary?
MARY	No, I think I've -
FRANK	Haven't drunk that yet, have you? Want something else? Whisky, gin, martini?
MARY	No thank you, I -
FRANK	What else have we got? (He crosses to drinks cabinet and looks in cupboard.)
WILLIAM	(jigging up and down again) Excuse me - I wonder if I could just -
FRANK	Yes, yes, of course. (He crosses to MARY and indicates the sofa.)

(MARY crosses and sits C. of sofa and WILLIAM sits L. end.)

(crossing back to drinks cabinet)   Sit down. Take a seat. Now then. Let's see. Orange juice, ginger ale, soda water, tonic water –

(MARY jumps up. WILLIAM follows.)

MARY   Oh, well –

FRANK   Tonic water?

(WILLIAM pulls MARY down and they sit.)

MARY   Thank you.

FRANK   Jolly good.   (He opens a bottle of tonic.)

WILLIAM   We were just saying, what a nice room this is?

FRANK   Room?

WILLIAM   Yes.

FRANK   Yes, I suppose it is. I've seen it before of course. (He crosses D.S. to L. of sofa.)   Here we are. Jolly good health.

WILLIAM   Cheers.

MARY   Thank you.

(FRANK gestures to WILLIAM and MARY to move up, which they do, and FRANK sits L. end of sofa.)

FRANK   You know, I'd just like to say this to you both and – er you can take this as you like. My wife and I – we've been married – well, it was our anniversary yesterday – for God knows how many years. And there are times when acrimony creeps in. That is to say – we both get on each other's wick. Now then, what I always say to myself at times like these is well, Frank, it's better than nothing. And the older you get the better it is and the bigger the nothing. So my advice is, stick it out. Stick it out. Don't do things now that you're going to regret when you get too old, like me, to want to do them any more. (Pause.)   And that's all I have to say on the matter. Cheers!

WILLIAM)
MARY   )   Cheers!

                    (FIONA enters from kitchen R. and crosses to L. of sofa.
                    WILLIAM and MARY rise. WILLIAM sits and pulls MARY
                    down.)

FIONA   Oh, hallo, is Frank looking after you alright? Dinner
                    won't be long –

FRANK   Ah, that's good news. All getting a bit peckish, I think,
                    aren't we? I certainly am.

FIONA   Good. Darling, you left your shoes on top of the stove.
                    I thought you might need them.   (She hands FRANK
                    his shoes.)

FRANK   Ah!

FIONA   What have you all been talking about, then? Anything
                    interesting?

FRANK   (significantly to WILLIAM and MARY)   No, no, no –
                    just er chatting.

FIONA   (loathe to leave them)   – Chatting – ? Well – yes –
                    Won't be too long now.   (She exits into kitchen R.)

                    (WILLIAM rises. MARY rises. WILLIAM sits. MARY sits.
                    WILLIAM rises.)

FRANK   Um.

WILLIAM   (hopping up and down a bit)   Excuse me. Do you
                    think I could just pop up and wash my hands?

FRANK   Oh, yes of course.   (He pulls WILLIAM down.)
                    I'd better give you the directions. Better explain the
                    geography to you.   (He pulls on a shoe, and places it
                    on the drinks table to tie up the lace.)

                    (WILLIAM moves the glasses to make more room, and
                    FRANK misinterprets the gesture and thinks that WILLIAM
                    is offering to do the lace up.)

                    Oh, that's very kind of you – just a loose bow. Well, you
                    go up one flight, there's a door on your left. Pass that.
                    Then you pass the door that's straight ahead of you as well.

Now after that, if you sort of follow the passage which
tends to double back on itself, if you see what I mean,
the second door on your left, after you've turned that
corner, is the bathroom. Ready for the other one, are
you?   (He puts the other foot on the table.)   If
you want the other thing, it's nearly obliquely opposite
it, on your right, as it were.

WILLIAM   Yes. Thank you.   (He rises.)

FRANK   (pulling WILLIAM down)   It's a bit of a brute to pull,
by the way. If it doesn't go first time, don't get into a
flap. The trick is – give a sharp, firm yank – count a
slow seven and then bash the cistern with the palm of
your hand, just to the left of the name plate. You can't
miss.

WILLIAM   Right.

FRANK   Have a good time.

WILLIAM   Right.   (He rises and exits rapidly U.L.)

(FRANK looks at MARY. She reacts nervously. He
moves to C. of sofa, next to MARY.)

FRANK   A lot of men get up to this sort of thing, you know. But it
blows over.

MARY   Does it?

FRANK   Almost invariably.

MARY   What does?

FRANK   If you're in any sort of trouble at all – you know the sort
of trouble I mean – please feel that you can come and chat
it over with me, or my wife. I won't try and pretend that
William isn't going to be a great asset to our department.
And it's my job, in so far as it's possible, to see he's
happy. But I think that includes you.

MARY   Thank you.

FRANK   My wife put me in the picture about you, you see.

MARY   Did she?

FRANK   Oh yes. We don't have any secrets between us. She told me all about your little meeting –

MARY   What meeting?

FRANK   Last night.

MARY   I didn't go to any meeting –

FRANK   No, no, no. Your meeting with her –

MARY   I was at home all last night. William was away you see –

FRANK   Home?

MARY   Watching television.

FRANK   Oh, were you? That's odd – I thought my wife said she –
            Oh, television? Ah, you didn't happen to see that
            programme about these three chaps –

MARY   Oh – yes, peculiar wasn't it?

WILLIAM   (entering U.L. and crossing D.S. to L. of sofa)   Found
            it first go.

FRANK   Oh, well done.

WILLIAM   While I was in there, I – er – took the liberty of easing
            the pin on your ball-cock.

FRANK   Well. As long as you enjoyed yourself.   (He rises to
            R. of WILLIAM.)   Look, I'll just nip into the kitchen
            now and see if the wife wants a hand.   (He pushes
            WILLIAM onto sofa and crosses to U.S. of sofa.)   You
            two feel perfectly free to – talk. You're a couple of
            sillies. I've a jolly good mind to bang your heads together.
            (He bangs their heads together, and goes out R., laughing.)

MARY   (rising and crossing to R. of WILLIAM)   William –

WILLIAM   Yes?

MARY   Mr Foster was just saying something very peculiar.

WILLIAM   What sort of thing?

MARY   Well, I don't know, but he seemed to be saying –

WILLIAM   Now what?

MARY   No, it's silly.   (She nibbles her nails.)

WILLIAM	I'm afraid you're being more incoherent than usual tonight, Mary. (He crosses U.S. to D.S. of kitchen door L.)
	(MARY crosses to his R.)
	I'm not following you at all.
	(WILLIAM goes to smack her hand, when TERESA enters from L. He changes the movement into a gesture of greeting. TERESA crosses to U.S. of her dining table.)
TERESA	Hallo. I've been – trying to get everything ready. I don't know what's happened to Bob, I'm sure.
MARY	Can we help?
TERESA	Well, no, I think I've done most of it now, thanks. Oh, I tell you what. If you're feeling strong, William, I wonder if you'd – (She holds out wine.)
WILLIAM	(crossing D.S. of table and taking bottle) Yes, of course. (He crosses to R. of dining table with bottle and corkscrew and tries to draw the cork.)
MARY	Got Benjamin off to sleep have you?
TERESA	Oh yes, he's alright. Not a sound. Want to have a peep at him?
MARY	Oh, could I? I'll be very quiet.
TERESA	It's alright. Once he's off, he's off. Through the kitchen and – oh, you'll find it.
MARY	(going) Right. (She crosses to kitchen doorway and exits into kitchen L.)
TERESA	(crossing to U.L. of WILLIAM and tapping him on shoulder) Can you manage?
WILLIAM	Oh yes. Yes, I've opened one or two in my time, I can tell you.
TERESA	Yes. (Pause. She crosses and sits on D.S. end of her dining table with feet on the chair.) I suppose that's where Bob is.
WILLIAM	Where?
TERESA	In the pub.

WILLIAM   Oh well, he might be. I've heard he enjoyed a drink. He's usually in the pub with that crowd from the office at lunchtimes. I've seen them all going in.   (He draws the cork and hands corkscrew to TERESA and crosses to her R.)

TERESA   (taking bottle from him and putting it back on the table) You don't drink at lunchtimes, then?

WILLIAM   Oh no. I'd be fast asleep. No, as a matter of fact, I drink very sparingly, altogether.

TERESA   (smiling)   How did you survive with Bob the other night, then?

WILLIAM   Other night?

TERESA   On that binge you both had?

WILLIAM   Binge? When was this?

TERESA   Couple of nights ago. When was it? Wednesday.

WILLIAM   Not Wednesday. I was in Scunthorpe on Wednesday.

TERESA   Scunthorpe?

WILLIAM   Yes. First Wednesday of every month. Always the same. Stay the night there. Visit our branch, look over their books. Don't know why it should be Wednesday, though, I'm sure. Always has been.

TERESA   Scunthorpe?

WILLIAM   Yes. Anything wrong?

TERESA   Have you ever been out for a drink with Bob?

WILLIAM   No. I said, I wasn't the drinking –

TERESA   Have you ever – discussed your marriage with Bob at all?

WILLIAM   Discussed it, how do you mean?

TERESA   Talked to him about it, in detail, you know what I mean.

WILLIAM   Certainly not, no. I don't believe in –

TERESA   (dangerously quiet)   Thank you. That's all I want to know. Thank you.   (She begins to stack BOB's cutlery and crockery back on to the tray.)   Well –

(WILLIAM watches fascinated as TERESA walks past him carrying the tray, opens the front door and tosses it fully laden, almost casually, into the street. She closes the door.)

WILLIAM   Terry, what are you doing?

TERESA   Would you pour me a drink please.

WILLIAM   Yes. Of course.   (He does so.)

TERESA   Well - that's it. As far as I'm concerned that's it.

WILLIAM   What's it?

TERESA   That - is - it.   (She takes a wine glass that WILLIAM has poured.)   Up his!   (She drains the glass.)

WILLIAM   Steady on.

TERESA   I'm going to get the supper.   (She jumps down, crosses L. of table, U.S. of table and then to R. of WILLIAM.)

                 (WILLIAM backs away D.L.)

                 (following WILLIAM)   I'm going to be absolutely madly, permissively modern. I am going to serve up the food and then, in the absence of our Lord and master, who is probably grovelling on the floor with some barmaid by now, we will all sit down and have a lovely chatty meal.

                 (WILLIAM sits D.L.)

                 (crossing U.S.)   That's what.

                 (MARY enters from kitchen L. to L. of TERESA.)

MARY   Isn't he beautiful?

TERESA   (hostilely)   Who's beautiful?

MARY   Benjamin.

                 (TERESA and MARY cross D.S.)

                 He's the dead spit of Bob, isn't he. Just like his daddy.

TERESA   Oh yes. The same squat, piggy little face, you mean.

MARY   Oh no, I didn't.

TERESA   Same nature, too, you know. Screams for what he wants till he gets it. He'll be a real little charmer when he grows up.

(MARY sits on R. arm of chair D.L.)

Just like his bloody father –   (She goes out L.)

MARY	What's wrong?
WILLIAM	Something very wrong, I'm afraid.
MARY	What?
WILLIAM	I don't know. Something to do with Scunthorpe.
MARY	Scunthorpe?
WILLIAM	And Bob's drinking. Then she threw a load of cutlery out of the front door –
MARY	Perhaps the dinner's spoilt.
WILLIAM	No. I rather think it's something more than that, somehow.
MARY	Oh.

(FIONA enters R. with a tray. Four dishes of avocado.)

FIONA   At last. You must have thought we'd gone to bed or something.   (She crosses to R. of dining table and puts down dishes.)   Now, I've put you, Mary, there. And William here.

(WILLIAM and MARY cross each other D.S. and cross to chairs U.S. of FIONA's dining table. MARY sits U.R. of table. WILLIAM crosses and holds FIONA's chair out for her. FIONA sits L. end of table. MARY jumps up and sits again. WILLIAM sits R. of FIONA.)

Do sit down. Frank's just digging us up something to drink from somewhere.

(WILLIAM and MARY both sit on swivel chairs which can swing through ninety degrees to take in BOB and TERESA's section as well.)

Now, I hope you like avocado. I know some people loathe them.   (She serves dishes to all four.)   Now this is all going to be terribly informal, so please don't expect anything elaborate. If I've forgotten to give you

anything just yell out. At the rate Frank's going he'll probably join us for coffee, but please do start.

(TERESA enters. WILLIAM and MARY swivel round. WILLIAM rises. TERESA has a tureen of soup.)

TERESA	It's alright. Don't get up.
MARY	Can we help?
TERESA	No. No, it's alright. I can manage perfectly, thank you. Just about. Everything's under control. I think. Just help yourselves - please help yourselves. Can you smell burning? (She sniffs.)
WILLIAM	Er -
TERESA	(rushing out) I knew it. I knew it. (She goes off into kitchen.)
MARY	(after a pause, starting to serve soup) Soup, William?
WILLIAM	(taking a bowl) Thank you. (He sniffs the soup.)
MARY	What are you doing?
WILLIAM	It smells of air freshener.
MARY	No.
WILLIAM	Definitely air freshener.
MARY	Well, try and eat it. She's gone to a lot of trouble.
WILLIAM	You know what happens to my stomach with badly cooked food.
MARY	Yes, dear. I know.

(FRANK enters with an opened bottle of wine. WILLIAM and MARY swivel.)

FRANK	Whoever put this cork in, did a good job. Been dancing round the kitchen trying to get it out.
FIONA	Sit down, darling.
FRANK	Right. (He sits.) Ah. Now then. What's this stuff?
FIONA	Avocado, you've had it before.

FRANK   Yes, I know I've had it before. Didn't recognize it that's all. Is it alright?

WILLIAM   Delicious.

MARY   Mmmm.

FRANK   Looks a bit off to me.

FIONA   Darling –

FRANK   Now then.   (He rises.)   Wine everybody? Mary?

MARY   Oh, no, thank you.

FRANK   (pouring her some all the same)   Oh, come on –

        (TERESA enters from the kitchen L. WILLIAM and MARY swivel.)

TERESA   That stove. That damned stove. I have asked Bob a hundred times – well I'm not waiting for him. He can damn well starve.

        (FRANK crosses to pour FIONA's wine.)

MARY   Is there anything the matter, Terry?

TERESA   Matter? Matter? Good heavens no. Come on then. Let's enjoy ourselves – Eat up –

MARY   Right. This looks delicious.   (She picks up her spoon.)

        (WILLIAM continues to gaze at his plate, dubiously.)

TERESA   William?

WILLIAM   Er – yes, thank you –

        (WILLIAM and MARY swivel.)

FRANK   (offering WILLIAM wine)   William?

WILLIAM   Thank you.

        (WILLIAM and MARY swivel.)

TERESA   I hope you enjoy this soup. I stood over it for hours.

        (WILLIAM and MARY dip their spoons in the soup.)

        I've put practically everything in it I could lay my hands on –

(WILLIAM and MARY each take a mouthful.)

Benjie helped me with it a little bit.

(WILLIAM and MARY choke.)

MARY   (recovering)   Aren't you having any?

TERESA   I couldn't face it just at the moment. Don't mind me.
              I'll just get drunk –

              (WILLIAM and MARY swivel. FRANK sits.)

FRANK   This doesn't taste like avocado at all to me. Tastes like
              pineapple chunks.

FIONA   If you're going to complain darling, the best thing to do is
              not to eat it.

FRANK   I'm not complaining. I prefer pineapple chunks, actually.

              (WILLIAM and MARY swivel.)

TERESA   How is it?

MARY   Wonderful.

WILLIAM   Very unusual.

TERESA   (picking up ladle)   I can't resist it. I'll have to try
              it.   (She sips the soup, replaces the ladle and stares
              at it.)   It tastes like anti-perspirant.

MARY   Oh.

WILLIAM   Well –

TERESA   Doesn't it taste like that to you? It must do –

MARY   No –

WILLIAM   Yes, it does.

TERESA   Then what the hell are you eating it for, for God's sake?
              Here, let me pour it back.   (She snatches their
              plates.)

MARY   (resisting)   No, no it's –

TERESA   Give it to me.   (A tug of war.)   Come on.
              (She gets their plates and pours the soup back into the
              tureen.)   Well that's that. End of the meal.

WILLIAM   Oh? Why is that?

TERESA   The chops are completely burnt and I don't know how you feel about raw potatoes.

WILLIAM   Ah.

MARY   Oh dear.

TERESA   (cheerfully)   Never mind. There's always the wine, isn't there? The least we can do is behave like civilized human beings. I don't know about you two but I'm going to enjoy myself.   (She starts to sing loudly and discordantly.)

            (WILLIAM and MARY sit appalled till she finishes and takes another swig of wine. WILLIAM and MARY swivel.)

FRANK   What have we got coming up after this then?

FIONA   Frigadella.

FRANK   Frigadella? Frozen stuff, eh?

FIONA   No, darling, it's veal and pork.

FRANK   Oh, well, I expect we'll recognize it when we see it. Talking of recognizing things, we had a little chap in the office once. Came from somewhere up North. Perkins was it? No, it was Porter – Porterhouse. Some name like that.

FIONA   Darling do eat.

FRANK   No, it was Carter. That's it. Billy Carter. Don't know where I got the name Porterhouse from. Anyway he came from up North. He had the most terrible wife. Little woman. Now in those days the Chairman was very keen to make it one big happy family. And that included the wives. Now it was just before the office Christmas party and he decided to put Mrs Carter in charge of the – no, it wasn't Carter. What was her name now – ?

FIONA   Darling, we are all simply panting for our second course.

            (WILLIAM and MARY swivel.)

TERESA   Did you ever hear that very funny story about the wife who came home unexpectedly and found her husband in

	bed with the baby sitter.
MARY	Oh!
WILLIAM	No I don't believe we have.
TERESA	Well, there they both were, you see. Him and this girl –
WILLIAM	Terry, I wonder if I could just –
TERESA	Both of them on the bed. At it for dear life – (The doorbell rings.) – and the wife just stands there and says –
WILLIAM	Isn't that the doorbell?
TERESA	The wife says – let it ring – says to her husband very sweetly –
WILLIAM	I think that was the doorbell.
TERESA	(sharply) Let it ring – she says to him, terribly sweetly, 'You can practise till you're blue in the face, darling, but you'll never get it right.' (MARY laughs nervously.)
WILLIAM	(appalled) Mary! (MARY stops laughing. WILLIAM and MARY swivel.)
FRANK	(slamming down his spoon, having suddenly remembered) Fraser! That was it. Mrs Fraser.
FIONA	Well done, darling. I'll get the rest. (She rises and picks up the tray from trolley.) (MARY also rises.) No, sit still Mary. I can manage.
FRANK	Anyway, now then. Mrs – I've forgotten what I was telling you about now.
WILLIAM	The office Christmas party.
FRANK	Oh yes. And Mrs –
MARY	Mrs Carter.
FRANK	Carter? That wasn't her name.

WILLIAM   Mrs Fraser.

FRANK   Fraser! That's it, Fraser. Yes, the Chairman decided to put Mrs – I don't think that was her name either, come to think of it. What was it now.

FIONA   (going out with the plates)   Darling, you really are becoming awfully tedious.

                (FIONA goes out to the kitchen. As she does so TERESA's doorbell rings. WILLIAM and MARY swivel.)

WILLIAM   (rising)   I think I'd better answer it.

TERESA   It's entirely up to you, Bill. I'm not answering anything. I'm going to enjoy my dinner.

                (FRANK polishes his cutlery thoughtfully on the tablecloth. BOB's singing is heard off. WILLIAM opens the door and recoils as BOB lunges in. He has a carrier bag with him.)

BOB   Well, well, all tucking in are we. Filling ourselves with goodies? Very nice too. Did you cook anything for me, love, or shall I go to the Café.

TERESA   Oh God!

BOB   Hallo, there's Mary the mouse. Hallo, Mary the mouse, how are you?

MARY   Hallo – Bob –

BOB   Well, then. How have things been going – ?
          (He shoves WILLIAM.)   Sit down, William, don't mind me –

                (WILLIAM does so.)

                All been telling dirty jokes, have we?

TERESA   Yes. I've heard some very dirty jokes, thank you.

BOB   I thought you might. I thought you'd soon ferret that out.

TERESA   Well I did.

BOB   Good.   (He turns his attention to the carrier bag.) Now then, what have we here?   (He starts to unload a number of tins of beer.)

                (WILLIAM and MARY swivel.)

FIONA	(entering from kitchen) First batch. (She puts two vegetable dishes down on the table.)
WILLIAM	Sure you can manage?
FIONA	Yes, thank you. Frank will give me a hand. Won't you, darling?
FRANK	What? Oh yes. You should have said. Should have said –
FIONA	It's fairly obvious, darling. I don't have to tell you, surely? You can see me, staggering in and out laden with dishes.
	(FRANK and FIONA go out. WILLIAM and MARY swivel.)
BOB	(opening can of beer and crossing D.S. to L. of TERESA) Who's for beer then? Eh? William, I know you'll have one?
WILLIAM	– Er, no thanks, Bob. Got the wine, thank you.
BOB	(aggressively) Come on. Have a beer. (He pours beer into WILLIAM's glass.)
	(WILLIAM covers glass with his hand.)
TERESA	Bob, we're having a meal. Either sit down or –
BOB	(crossing to R. of TERESA) Mary. Mary will have a beer. Won't you, Mary?
MARY	Oh, no, no – thanks –
BOB	Well, she won't. (He nods at TERESA.) She thinks beer's a bit common actually. You know what she likes? Egg Nog. Egg Nog – known as alcoholic custard –
TERESA	Bob, shut up.
BOB	Why should I shut up. I'm offering our friends a drink, that's all. (He leans over MARY.) Do excuse her manners. Her education was not what it should have been –
TERESA	(dangerously quiet) I warn you, I shall throw something.
BOB	Oh, that'll be good. They'll enjoy that. (He crosses

to U.S. of WILLIAM.)   She's got a good aim. Hit a
wall with a plate of baked beans at twenty paces.
(He swings beer can over WILLIAM's head.)

(WILLIAM ducks.)

(crossing D.S. to D.L. of dining table)   You don't
believe me? I've seen her do it – Right, four beers, it
is, then.   (He crosses U.S. to sideboard.)

(WILLIAM and MARY swivel. FIONA enters from kitchen
R. followed by FRANK. They cross L., U.S. of table.
FIONA crosses to her place, puts dish down and takes
plates from FRANK.)

FIONA   Do stop fussing, darling. They're not as hot as all that.
I think this has turned out alright. I hope so.

FRANK   (crossing U.S. of table and sitting R. of table)   Smells
a bit off to me.

FIONA   (sighing)   There's eggs and bacon in the pantry.
You've no idea, William, the number of times he's actually
got up from the dinner table and gone off to fry himself
eggs and things. It really is terribly disheartening.
(She places the dish down and starts to serve it onto
plates.)

(WILLIAM and MARY swivel.)

BOB   (crossing D.S. with beer and pouring it into MARY's
glass)   Here we are, Mary. One for you.

MARY   No really, Bob, I –

TERESA   Bob, she doesn't want any –

BOB   (leaning over MARY)   Well, she's having it whether
she likes it or not. I can't sit here drinking alone. It's
bloody unsociable –

WILLIAM   Now listen, Bob, I don't think you should –

BOB   Oh shut up.   (He crosses to window R.)

TERESA   You really are a pig, aren't you. A rude drunk pig.

(MARY and WILLIAM rise.)

MARY   I really think we ought to go –

TERESA   (rising and pushing WILLIAM and MARY down and
              crossing to U.S. of her chair)   No, don't go. If
              anyone's going, it's the pig.

BOB   Me?

TERESA   Yes, you.

              (WILLIAM and MARY swivel.)

FIONA   William, you know it's terrible having a husband with
              absolutely no palate.

WILLIAM   Oh dear. I'm so sorry.

              (WILLIAM and MARY swivel.)

BOB   If I want to stay here, I shall stay here.   (He moves
              closer to TERESA, half menacing.)

              (WILLIAM and MARY swivel.)

FIONA   That's why Frank doesn't really enjoy these occasions.

FRANK   Oh yes, I do. I'm enjoying it very much.

MARY   Oh yes. So am I.

              (WILLIAM and MARY swivel.)

TERESA   (picking up soup ladle)   I'm warning you, Bob.

WILLIAM   (apprehensively)   Terry, I don't think I should –

TERESA   Bob –

BOB   (moving closer to TERESA)   Go on then, I dare you –

              (WILLIAM and MARY swivel.)

FRANK   Just a minute. You interrupted my story about Mrs
              Whatsername. Now then –   (He pauses for thought.)

              (WILLIAM and MARY swivel. TERESA snatches up the
              soup ladle and swings at BOB with it. He ducks and
              catches her wrist. They struggle silently. WILLIAM and
              MARY watch horrified. WILLIAM and MARY swivel.)

              She was put in charge of refreshments for the office
              Christmas party – and what do you think she gave us?
              Have a guess.

(WILLIAM and MARY swivel. BOB forces TERESA to drop the ladle. She kicks him. She runs downstage centre where he catches her. WILLIAM and MARY swivel.)

Give up? Hot pot! What do you think of that?

(WILLIAM and MARY swivel. TERESA bites BOB and escapes. He yells and chases her round the table. WILLIAM and MARY swivel.)

Christmas office party with the guests weaving in and out with steaming bowls of hot pot.

(WILLIAM and MARY swivel.)

MARY	Is anything the matter?
WILLIAM	Bob, I don't think this is really –

(TERESA rushes into the kitchen pursued by BOB. WILLIAM and MARY swivel.)

FRANK   The managing director got some all down his shirt front during the tango.

(WILLIAM and MARY swivel. TERESA screams from off R.)

BOB   (off)   Bitch!

(WILLIAM and MARY swivel.)

FRANK   Well, he turns on this woman Mrs Taylor – Taylor! That's it. Taylor – and he says, now let me get this right, he says –

(WILLIAM and MARY swivel.)

TERESA   (off)   Damn you.

(WILLIAM and MARY swivel.)

FRANK   Well he really lets her have it. And Mrs Taylor, who's had a few herself by then, says – how did she put it now –

(WILLIAM and MARY swivel.)

TERESA   (backing on from the kitchen)   Keep away, Bob – keep away. I'm warning you.

WILLIAM   Bob, for heaven's sake –

(BOB follows TERESA on from the kitchen. WILLIAM and

MARY swivel.)

FRANK   I know what she said –

(WILLIAM and MARY swivel. TERESA picks up the soup tureen.)

WILLIAM   Terry!

MARY   No!

WILLIAM   (leaping between TERESA and BOB)   Bob, I – Terry – no!

(TERESA throws the soup. It hits WILLIAM square on. He staggers to his chair, and sits. WILLIAM and MARY swivel.)

FRANK   That's right! Mrs Taylor says –

(TERESA rushes out of the front door. BOB follows her laughing.)

Mrs Taylor says – you're wet!

WILLIAM   (laughing appreciatively)   Oh! Very good –

FRANK   No, no. You are wet.

WILLIAM   Oh. Oh, dear, there appears to be a drip.

FRANK   Drip?

FIONA   Darling, you haven't left the shower on again?

FRANK   Of course not. Anyway, William isn't sitting under the bathroom. He's under the – er – other place.

(They all gaze towards the ceiling.)

CURTAIN

ACT II

Scene One

Set as in Act I, Scene 1 except the two R. seats of the settee now match the
PHILLIPS' decor and the L. seat matches the FOSTER's decor.

Saturday morning. A sign hangs on the inside of TERESA's front door saying
'Goodbye Forever'.

	(BOB enters from R. and crosses to C.)
BOB	(calling) Terry! Terry! (He stares round, sees the sign and slumps, clad only in his trousers, in the armchair D.L.)
	(FRANK bursts in U.L. as before. He reaches the timer on table R. of C. chair and pulls up short, delighted that it has not rung. He looks at his own watch congratulating himself. He looks at the timer again for confirmation. His smile fades. He clicks it, shakes it, listens to it – finally bangs it. He is very put out. He strides off into the kitchen L. As he does so BOB's doorbell rings. BOB is startled, then smiles rather smugly. He rises and crosses U.S. to front door U.R.)
	(flinging door open) Home again then, eh? Wouldn't kindly old mother shelter little red riding drawers from the big bad – eh – (It is MARY.)
MARY	(stepping in and stepping back again) Hallo.
BOB	Come in. Do come in.
MARY	Thank you. (She enters and crosses D.S. of step.)
	(BOB slams door.)
	(jumping) Is er – (She peers round.)
BOB	(crossing close to MARY on her L.) A little chillier this morning, don't you think? Though it might brighten later. Don't like the look of those clouds though, do you. Could have a little rain, don't you agree? Or even snow.

	You know what they say - red sky in the morning, shepherds warning. Red sky at night your roof is alight. What can I do for you?
MARY	I -
BOB	(courteously) Sit down.
MARY	(crossing D.S., R. of sofa and sitting on R. end) Thank you.
	(BOB also re-seats himself D.L.)
BOB	Can I - do anything for you?
MARY	No. I just wanted a word with Terry, you see.
BOB	She's not here.
MARY	No. Will she be back?
BOB	It's unlikely.
MARY	Oh, I see.
BOB	All the signs seem to indicate that she's gone for good.
MARY	Oh.
BOB	She's walked out before, you see, but I've been making a quick inventory and this time she seems to have taken quite a comprehensive collection of essential items with her. One nightie, one toothbrush, at least two sets of under- wear, a long playing record of Benjamin Britten's War Requiem and the baby.
MARY	But what made her go?
BOB	I don't know. She may have eloped with the editor of the Guardian.
MARY	Who's he?
BOB	Yes. Failing that, I repeat, what can I do for you?
MARY	It's just - if we could help in any way?
BOB	Help?
MARY	Well, last night - That soup and things - I just thought that if there was anything that William and I could do to help - ?

BOB	No. That's all cleaned up, thank you.
MARY	I didn't mean that.
BOB	Didn't you?
MARY	I meant – help. You know.
BOB	That's very nice of you.
MARY	(warming) I mean, I thought if you and William were going to be working together, we ought –
BOB	We ought to be able to get together. Quite.
MARY	Yes.
BOB	Where is he?
MARY	Mmm?
BOB	Why hasn't he come with you?
	(MARY does not reply.)
	He knows you're here, doesn't he?
MARY	Well, I –
BOB	Oh. He doesn't feel as strongly as you, the urge to help? Is that it?
MARY	Well, we talked about it last night – only he felt we shouldn't interfere –
BOB	Ah.
MARY	This was my idea. William always says I'm too – retiring. That I must get interested, talk to people, you see. Because it's important to talk to people, isn't it? Making social contact is essential. If you're going to have people coming round and drinking sherry and things you must be able to converse with them. And then I thought, well, perhaps the first thing to do is to get to know you and Terry. Perhaps talk over problems. That sort of thing. Just generally sort of help. I mean, that's what we're on this earth for, isn't it?
BOB	Good point.
MARY	Thank you.

BOB   Yes.   (He rises and crosses to U.S. of armchair C.)
You're right. Now, there's a broom in the kitchen
cupboard and I think you'll find the mop right next to it.

MARY   What – ?

BOB   No, I'll tell you what.   (He crosses R, U.S. of sofa
and leans over back of sofa.)   Let's not take advantage
of friendship. Twenty-five pence an hour, how's that?
Thirty-five when you're using the vacuum cleaner because
that's pretty heavy.   (He crosses towards kitchen L.)

MARY   (rising)   I may come back.

BOB   Sit down.

MARY   No, I really must be –

BOB   (fiercely)   Sit down.

              (MARY does so. Startled.)

MARY   Don't think you can talk to me the way you talk to Terry.

BOB   I wouldn't dream of it.   (He crosses to R. of sofa.)
Mind you, I'd hate you to go away feeling that I'm
ungrateful. I'm not. I'll tell you what, cheer up.
(He sits R. of MARY.)   I'll go and put a shirt on, you
go and make us some coffee and then we'll both sit down
here and I'll tell you all about our marriage. How would
that suit you?

MARY   No –

BOB   No pleasing you, is there? Alright, you tell me about
your problems.

MARY   I haven't got any problems.

BOB   Never mind, we'll soon invent some.   (He pats MARY
on knee, rises and crosses D.S. of C. armchair to kitchen
doorway L.)   This could be fun.

MARY   (rising)   I ought to go.

BOB   Make the coffee – You may even find a cup on the
draining board if you dig deep enough.   (He exits
into bedroom L.)

(FRANK enters with timer, screwdriver and a coffee from kitchen R., crosses to L. of double doors, takes chair and moves it to U.S. of table L. and sits.)

MARY   (sitting)   But I -

(FRANK drops the timer into his coffee and attempts to fish it out with the screwdriver. The doorbell rings. He rises and exits U.L. MARY rises and crosses U.S. towards front door U.R. BOB appears in kitchen doorway. He enters and catches MARY creeping towards the front door. He pulls the belt from his trousers, brandishing it threateningly.)

BOB   Hey!

(MARY freezes.)

Coffee, coffee, coffee.

(MARY crosses L. and exits into kitchen D.S. of BOB. BOB exits into bedroom L. FRANK appears in hallway with pram followed by TERESA.)

FRANK   This is very - unexpected, Terry.

TERESA   Yes. I suppose it is.   (She enters U.L. and crosses to U.L. of sofa.)   Sorry.

FRANK   No, no - a pleasure. A pleasure. Baby'll be alright in the hall, will he? Must say he looks pretty snug and tucked away.   (He leans over the carrycot.) Oo-hoo!

TERESA   Oh, yes, but let him sleep.

(FRANK enters U.L. and crosses to U.S. of C. armchair.)

Must have been the bus journey. As soon as we got on he dropped off.

FRANK   Dropped off?

TERESA   To sleep.

FRANK   Ah. Now, then. Do sit down.

TERESA   (sitting L. end of sofa)   Thanks.

FRANK   Can I get you some coffee?

TERESA   No, thank you.

FRANK   (crossing D.S. to L. of armchair)   I would offer you
                mine, but it seems to have a hair-spring in it. Now,
                what can I do for you?   (He stands a bit awkwardly,
                wondering why she has come.)

                (TERESA broods for a moment.)

TERESA   I was on the bus you see –

FRANK   Were you? Yes. Nothing like a bus ride on a Saturday
                morning –

TERESA   I was on my way to my mother's –

FRANK   Ah! Were you? Nice the way you young people
                communicate with your parents.

TERESA   And I thought I must talk to someone. Anyone. Then we
                passed the end of your road and I thought of you. So I
                got off.

FRANK   Glad you did. Glad you did. Still, your mother will be
                a bit disappointed. I suppose you sent old Bob on ahead,
                hm?

TERESA   I've left him, Frank.

FRANK   Where?

TERESA   We've separated, you see. At least I have.

FRANK   (stunned)   Good Lord.   (He crosses and sits in
                armchair C.)   Good Lord – I don't know what to say –
                I – Good Lord, good grief. But this is shocking news,
                Terry. Absolutely shocking.

TERESA   I don't know who this other woman is, but –

FRANK   Woman?

TERESA   (muttering)   He's got another woman.

FRANK   Another another one? Must be catching.

TERESA   What?

FRANK   Nothing. You've no idea who she is, I suppose?

TERESA   No idea.

FRANK	Fiona'll be shattered you know.
TERESA	Will she?
FRANK	Oh absolutely. Always been particularly fond of you both.
TERESA	So I'm being boringly conventional and running home to mother.
FRANK	No, no, no. You get on alright with her, do you?
TERESA	I shouldn't think so. We'll be at each other's throats in five minutes. I think she prefers Bob, really. I'm too much like my father.
FRANK	Well, you'll have to talk to him, then.
TERESA	He left us in 1953.
FRANK	Ah. Listen, Terry, are you absolutely certain about this?
TERESA	Oh yes. He's been gone nineteen years.
FRANK	No, I mean, you and Bob. (He rises and crosses to L. of armchair.) You're such a jolly little couple – jolly little flat – jolly little baby. All your future in front of you. (He crosses to L. of TERESA.) Oh, I know we all make jokes about Bob being the office Romeo –
TERESA	Really? I didn't know.
FRANK	No, no, no. Men's jokes. Nothing serious.
TERESA	This is serious.
FRANK	Yes, of course. Are you quite sure of your facts? Got any concrete evidence?
TERESA	Enough. Staying out till all hours in the morning –
FRANK	Yes, well, that isn't really evidence. (He crosses and sits C.) I mean, take me for instance. I could turn round and say – where on earth is Fiona at the moment. And the answer would be – I haven't the slightest idea. But I certainly don't imagine she's in bed with the chap next door. More probably at the hair-dressers.

TERESA	Presumably she doesn't stop at the hairdressers till three o'clock in the morning, though.
FRANK	No, I don't think she does.
TERESA	Well, then?
FRANK	She has been out till that time, though.
TERESA	Has she?
FRANK	Lord, yes. Not frequently, mind you, but occasionally. Why only the other day – when was it – last – wedding anniversary – Wednesday, she was out till all hours.
TERESA	Wednesday?
FRANK	Yes, Wednesday. Really very late.
TERESA	Wednesday?
FRANK	Still you don't want to talk about me – it's your problems we're after.
TERESA	Wednesday?
FRANK	Tell you what I'll do. I'll have a word with old Bob – see if I can get to the bottom of it. He'll have to listen to me.
TERESA	Yes!
FRANK	(picking up the phone and dialling) Yes! I'll read him the riot act, shall I?
TERESA	Oh! No.
FRANK	No? Oh, well. (He replaces the phone.) Second thoughts are very often best. (He rises.) Look are you sure I can't get you something to drink?
TERESA	(thoughtfully) No thanks.
FRANK	Tea? Coffee? (He crosses to L. of TERESA.) It's all bubbling away out there.
TERESA	Thanks.
FRANK	You will?
TERESA	Yes, please.

(FRANK crosses D.S. of sofa and turns at D.R. corner.)
Oh, yes!

FRANK   Yes! Black or white?

TERESA   Black please.

FRANK   (going to leave again, then turning)   Coffee?

TERESA   Yes, please.

FRANK   Right.   (He exits into kitchen R.)

(MARY enters from kitchen L. and crosses D.S. of sofa
with duster and dustpan. She kneels D.S. of sofa and
starts tidying. BOB enters from bedroom L. and crosses to
C. TERESA takes out and lights cigarette.)

BOB   What are you doing?

MARY   (startled)   Oh. Just having a little dust.

BOB   Where's the coffee?

MARY   You won't get any if you talk like that.

(BOB crosses to U.S. of sofa and leans over back watching
MARY dust.)

BOB   Look, would you mind leaving my house alone?

MARY   I'm only cleaning up a little.

BOB   Well don't. My wife spent a great deal of time and
           trouble accumulating that dust. And in five minutes you've
           undone years of her work.

MARY   (moving to R. of sofa on her knees)   Don't be silly.

BOB   You're a home wrecker. That's what you are –

MARY   You don't want a dirty house.

BOB   Why not?

MARY   Well it's – dirty.

BOB   Look. Do me a favour and make the bloody coffee.

(MARY rises and crosses to C.S. BOB crosses R. of sofa.)

MARY   (getting angry for her)   You are very, very, very rude.

(She turns and crosses to U.S. of sofa.)   I don't know
how Terry puts up with you –   Oh.

BOB   She doesn't any more, does she?   (He laughs.)
Coffee, coffee!

(MARY exits into kitchen L., followed by BOB. FIONA
comes in from the front door.)

FIONA   Hallo, Terry. How are you?

TERESA   Oh, quite well –

FIONA   I wondered what that heaving package in the hall was.
It's your baby, isn't it?

TERESA   Probably.

FIONA   Sweet.   (She crosses and puts dress box, bag and
gloves on table L.)   What a simply dolly pushchair.
Beautifully bright and gay –

TERESA   It's a carry-cot actually. On wheels.

FIONA   Oh, is that what it is? Super. Sweetie, you won't mind
my saying so but it does look as if he's drooled just a teeny
bit on the carpet –

TERESA   Oh. Yes, he often does that –

FIONA   Oh, it doesn't matter as long as he's all right. Fearful
old carpet anyway, probably brightens it up.

FRANK   (entering from kitchen R with cup and crossing to U.L. of
sofa)   Ah, Fiona. Thank God you're here. I'm
afraid you're going to have to brace yourself –

FIONA   Why?

FRANK   Terry's just dropped a bombshell.

FIONA   Has she?

FRANK   Bob's got another woman –

FIONA   Another one?

FRANK   A lover, dear. A love affair.

FIONA   Oh. Well – I'm – absolutely amazed.

FRANK   They've split up, you see.

FIONA	Really?
FRANK	Terry's walked out.
FIONA	(crossing to L. of armchair C.) I can't believe you'd do that –
TERESA	No. Well I haven't actually –
FRANK	Haven't? But I thought you said –
TERESA	I've been thinking it over. You were absolutely right –
FRANK	Was I? Oh – good.
TERESA	After all, why should I give him up. We keep saying it's a love affair but it probably wasn't anything of the sort –
FRANK	Quite –
FIONA	Quite –
TERESA	Knowing Bob – it's far more likely to be some rich, old boot he decided to take out for a giggle –
FRANK	(amused) Rich, old boot. Yes –
TERESA	(rising to R. of FRANK) You've been a big help. Thank you Frank –
FRANK	Not at all – least I could do –
TERESA	Well – I must dash. (She crosses U.S. to double doors.) Bye then.
FIONA	Bye!
TERESA	(to FIONA) Sorry about the mess – in the hall.
FIONA	(crossing U.S. to L. of steps) Perfectly alright.
TERESA	You won't mind if I leave you to clean it up, will you? (She blows FIONA a kiss and goes out into the hall, closing the door behind her.)
FRANK	Good morning's work. Good morning's work.
FIONA	Darling, what's going on?
FRANK	(pacing) Tell you in a second. This needs a little more thought.
FIONA	Oh? (She crosses to table L. and opens dress box.)

	Darling, I bought that dress by the way.
FRANK	Right.
FIONA	It looks simply ghastly on –
FRANK	Good.
FIONA	But I bought it anyway.
FRANK	Great.
FIONA	I'll tell you what, I'll put it on. You can tell me what you think.
FRANK	Right.
FIONA	Everything alright?
FRANK	Fine.

(FIONA goes out into the hall with an apprehensive look at FRANK. FRANK comes to a decision, crosses to phone and starts dialling.)

MARY	(entering from kitchen with BOB's coffee)　　　Here you are then, you don't – oh! – Bob!

(There is no reply, then BOB starts singing off, in the bathroom.)

BOB	Bless this house, dear Lord, we pray, Now my wife has gone away.

(MARY, disapproving, puts down the mug and starts dusting. MARY's phone rings. She looks at it for a moment, uncertainly. She glances off, but there's no sign of BOB. She answers it, uncertainly. She is obviously far from happy using the telephone.)

MARY	Hallo.
FRANK	Hallo.
MARY	Hallo.
FRANK	Hallo – Hallo –
MARY	Mr Phillips' residence.
FRANK	Who's that? His maid?

MARY	No, it's me.
FRANK	Who's me?
MARY	Mary. Mary Featherstone.
FRANK	Mary Featherstone?
MARY	I think Mr Phillips is in the bathroom at present.
FRANK	Mary Featherstone?
MARY	Who is that talking please?
FRANK	What are you doing?
MARY	When?
FRANK	Doing there? What are you doing there?
MARY	Dusting.
FRANK	What?
MARY	Dusting. Housework and things –
FRANK	My God –
MARY	Beg your pardon?
FRANK	Look, is Bob there?
MARY	I think he's just finishing getting dressed.
FRANK	Great heavens above.
MARY	Hallo – Could you tell me who's talking please?
FRANK	What?
MARY	Could you tell me your name?
FRANK	No. Wrong number. Sorry, wrong number –
MARY	Can I give him a message at all?
FRANK	No, no –
MARY	Who shall I say telephoned?
FRANK	Er – Mr – er – Mr – er – Mr Carrycot. I'll call back. Goodbye. (He slams down the phone.) Good grief. (He sits in armchair C.)

BOB	(entering from bathroom L. and crossing to U.S. of C. armchair drying his hands) Who was that?
MARY	(replacing the receiver she is still holding) A Mr Carrycot I think he said –
BOB	Oh yes? What did he want?
MARY	He said he'd call back. (She crosses U.S. to U.S. of sofa.)
BOB	Never heard of him. Perhaps it's my wife's solicitor. Or possibly the editor of the Guardian.
MARY	(impressed) Oh.

(BOB exits into bedroom L. FRANK dials. MARY crosses to table R. and puts papers into folder.)

FRANK   Hallo, is that William Featherstone ... oh, this is Frank Foster here ... yes, good morning to you ... hope I haven't caught you in the middle of anything ... You were what? ... lagging the pipes were you? ... jolly good ... wish I could say the same ... Look, listen William ... er ... Mary isn't there with you, is she ... oh ... no, no it doesn't matter ... you don't happen to know where she is, do you ... ? No, I don't want to talk to her, no ... I just wondered if you knew where she was, that's all ... yes, probably, probably walking somewhere, yes ...

(MARY picks up coffee and crosses D.S. of sofa and exits into kitchen L.)

Listen William something's cropped up here – in the kitchen – yes ... the sink. You don't happen to know anything about – U-bends do you ... ? It's just that we appear to have come up against a blockage ...

(FIONA enters in her new dress.)

Will you? That's very good of you. Sorry to interrupt your – er – lagging but I'd be – about ten minutes? Five? Splendid. Bye-bye.   (He puts phone down. He does not notice FIONA.)   Disastrous.

FIONA   I think that's rather brutal, darling.

FRANK	Absolutely disastrous.
FIONA	What if it were shorter?
FRANK	At this rate, my whole department is liable to splinter into a dozen pieces. I mean, one's heard of the permissive society, but one doesn't expect to find it running through one's own department. I don't know what's got into them all.
FIONA	(crossing U.S. to doors U.L.) I don't know what you're talking about, darling.
FRANK	All of them. The lot of them. (He rises and crosses U.S. to L. of FIONA.) You included.

(FIONA goes towards the door.)

My God, you're not going out again, are you? |
FIONA	I thought I'd take this off as you don't like it.
FRANK	I have a little matter to discuss with you –
FIONA	Really?
FRANK	Yes. (He guides FIONA D.S., R. of armchair.) Sit down –
FIONA	(slightly apprehensive) Darling, don't start getting all paternal –
FRANK	Sit down please.

(FIONA sits in armchair C.)

(standing to R. of FIONA)   I think I'm owed an explanation – |
FIONA	(rising) Well, I really do have a lot –
FRANK	Wednesday night.
FIONA	(sitting) Wednesday night?
FRANK	Last Wednesday night.
FIONA	Yes?
FRANK	Where were you?
FIONA	I was – I was – well, I – I told you.

FRANK   You told me you were out with Mary. Mary Featherstone.

FIONA   Oh, did I?

FRANK   Point one. And this I tended to overlook at the time.
            When the Featherstone's were round here on Thursday I
            mentioned this – so called meeting to Mary. She denied
            all knowledge of it –

FIONA   Did she?

FRANK   Yes. As I say. I took the matter no further. If for some
            reason you were doing something on Wednesday night that
            you didn't want me to know about, fair enough. No
            business of mine.

FIONA   That's – very sporting of you, darling.   (She rises and
            crosses to table L.)

FRANK   However, after Terry left this morning I phoned the
            Phillips house, and all is now clear to me. I now
            understand what it was you were trying to conceal on
            Wednesday night. And it is a very serious matter.

FIONA   (turning and facing FRANK)   I see.

FRANK   Quite honestly, dear, I'm rather disappointed in you.

FIONA   I suppose you must be.

FRANK   Why you should choose to conspire to conceal this rather
            sordid business from me, I don't know. Deliberately
            covering up, and rather badly at that –

FIONA   I thought – you might be hurt, I suppose –

FRANK   Well, I am. I am hurt –   (He crosses to L. of FIONA
            and examines label.)   You've got a label hanging off
            you, did you know? I am very hurt.

FIONA   Yes, darling.

FRANK   I mean surely we can share these things, together.

FIONA   Share them?

FRANK   These intimacies?

FIONA   Oh, well. It's not usual, surely –

FRANK   I know. You women. Thick as thieves.   (He crosses

U.S. to doors U.L.)   Well, I think I'm going to put some trousers on before William comes –

FIONA   (crossing U.S. to steps D.L. of FRANK)   What do you want me to do?

FRANK   You? You're alright dressed as you are, aren't you?

FIONA   No, I mean about us.

FRANK   Us? Don't quite follow you. Make us a drop more coffee if you like. That'd be a help.   (He exits U.L.)

FIONA   Oh Lord.   (She picks up coffee cups and exits into kitchen R.)

(MARY enters from kitchen L. and crosses D.S., L. of armchair with vacuum cleaner. She carries it to D.R. of sofa and looks for a plug and finally crawls under table D.R. TERESA enters U.R., sees vacuum cleaner gliding across floor, picks up tray from Welsh dresser and crosses D.R. and bangs it on table.)

TERESA   I'm back!

(MARY pokes her head out from under table. TERESA crosses and leans against table U.S. of MARY.)

Oh. Hallo.

MARY   Hallo, Terry.

TERESA   What are you doing here, for heaven's sake? Have you taken up charring or something?

MARY   I thought I might be able to help, you see.

TERESA   Help?

MARY   I mean after last night – the soup and so on.

TERESA   Oh, I see. Well, jolly nice of you.   (She crosses D.S. of sofa to C.)   I shouldn't do any more, this place is a job for life.   (She crosses U.S., L. of armchair C. and sees papers on table and crosses R., U.S. of sofa to U.S. of table R.)   – Hell's bloody bells, who's been at this lot?

MARY   Oh.   (She comes out from under table and rises to L. of TERESA.)   I think I just straightened –

TERESA	Oh, no. They're in a fine old muck now.
MARY	I'm sorry, have I - ?
TERESA	It's just I had them all sorted out, you see, love. They're all my press cuttings. All the articles I clip out from papers. I had birth control, famine relief and chemical warfare all in separate piles. Now they're all in a bloody jumble -

(FIONA enters from kitchen R. crosses to phone and dials.)

MARY	I'm terribly sorry -
TERESA	Oh Lord, all my letters are in here, too.
MARY	Letters?
TERESA	Copies of the ones I send to the editor of the Guardian - that's all -
MARY	Oh -

(TERESA answers the phone. MARY crosses to her R.)

TERESA	Hallo -

(FIONA gives a huge sigh of annoyance.)

(infuriated)   Pervert!

(FIONA drops phone and exits rapidly into kitchen R. TERESA slams down phone and crosses back to table R. MARY backs away L. BOB enters from kitchen L. and stands in doorway. MARY and TERESA look at him.)

BOB	Well, well, well.
TERESA	Hallo. (She crosses to U.R. corner of sofa.)

(TERESA and BOB face each other. MARY stands, fascinated.)

BOB	Forget something, did you?
TERESA	No.
BOB	Oh. Thought you might have popped back for alimony.
TERESA	(studying him. After a pause) You know, deep down inside, you're really rotten, aren't you?

BOB   You should know.

TERESA   God. I know.

BOB   Where's Benjy?

TERESA   Asleep.

BOB   Oh. Come here, then.

TERESA   Oh no.

BOB   Come here.

TERESA   No.   (Pause.)   You come here.

(MARY, who knows she ought to leave, can't. She's riveted.)

BOB   Alright.   (He moves to TERESA.)

(MARY retreats a pace, nervously, expecting violence. BOB reaches TERESA and faces her. His hand goes slowly to the back of her head and he takes her hair. MARY crosses to L. of BOB.)

(gently)   Silly cow.

TERESA   (the same)   Bastard.

(BOB and TERESA embrace. FIONA's doorbell rings. FIONA enters from kitchen R. and crosses L. and exits U.L. TERESA crosses D.S. of BOB, takes his hand and draws him across L., D.S. of MARY to kitchen doorway.)

(turning just before they exit)   Try not to wake Benjamin, love, won't you.

(BOB and TERESA exit into bedroom L. MARY crosses and leans on table R. WILLIAM enters U.L. brandishing a monkey wrench and crosses D.S. FIONA follows to his R.)

WILLIAM   Came round as quickly as I could –   (He waves wrench.)   This will do the trick.

FIONA   Oh?

WILLIAM   Have you fixed up in no time.

FIONA   Good. Thank you.   (Pause.)   My husband won't be a moment.

WILLIAM	Ah. Coping with the emergency, is he?
FIONA	Well, he's just putting on some trousers.
WILLIAM	Oh, I see. I hope I haven't called at an inconvenient time?
FIONA	No, not at all. Do sit down.

(WILLIAM sits in armchair C. FIONA crosses to D.S. of sofa. MARY picks up vacuum cleaner and crosses D.S. of sofa and then U.S., L. of armchair C. and exits into kitchen L.)

WILLIAM	May I take this opportunity of thanking you on behalf of my wife and myself for a delightful meal the other evening.
FIONA	Thank you.
WILLIAM	Thank you.

(A pause. FIONA smiles awkwardly at WILLIAM. He smiles back.)

That's a very attractive dress, if I may say so.

FIONA	Oh. Do you think so. Thank you.
WILLIAM	And brand new on today, unless I'm very much mistaken.
FIONA	Yes?
WILLIAM	Yes. I've spotted your little label –
FIONA	Oh that, yes.
WILLIAM	Overlooked that, hadn't you?
FIONA	No, actually, I left it on deliberately –
WILLIAM	Oh?
FIONA	I've tried it without, but I've come to the conclusion that I prefer the dress with the label on.
WILLIAM	Oh. I'm sorry, in that case.
FIONA	Quite alright. (She sits L. end of sofa.) I wonder if you could tell me something.
WILLIAM	I'll have a go.
FIONA	I want to ask you a theoretical question. It's purely

theoretical, mark you. I just want to know how you think you'd react.

WILLIAM   Alright. Fire ahead.

FIONA   If you – er –   If you found out that your wife was having an affair with another man, how would you react?

WILLIAM   What an extraordinary question.

FIONA   Yes, it is rather, isn't it?

WILLIAM   I mean, Mary would never dream of it –

FIONA   Of course not, I did say it's theoretical.

WILLIAM   I see.   (He considers.)   Well –

FIONA   I mean, do you for instance think you'd say – I'm rather disappointed in you. You might have shared it with me. Something like that?

WILLIAM   No. I don't think I'd say that. Hit her – perhaps? Sorry I can't be more help. I've had no real experience of that sort of situation.

FIONA   Nor have I –

            (FRANK enters U.L. and crosses D.S. to L. of WILLIAM. He claps his hands expectantly. WILLIAM rises.)

FRANK   Ah.

            (FIONA starts nervously.)

            Sorry. Hallo there, William. Nice of you to drop round.

WILLIAM   I was just saying – I came as soon as I could.

FRANK   I'm glad you did. Now the first thing is we must all have a drink and   (He pushes WILLIAM down and crosses U.S. to drinks cabinet.)   then we must sit down and have a talk –

            (FIONA crosses U.S. to L. of FRANK. FRANK hands her sherry.)

FIONA   Yes, well I'll just pop upstairs, darling, and –

FRANK   No, no, no. Need you here with us. Sit down.

FIONA   Well, I really –

FRANK	Sit down. (He guides FIONA back to sofa.)
	(FIONA sits with sherry.)
	(crossing U.S. to drinks cabinet and picking up sherry) You've got to have a drink. We've all got to have a drink –
WILLIAM	Well, it's a bit early, but still –
FRANK	I absolutely insist. (He crosses D.S. to R. of WILLIAM and hands him sherry.) Here we are then.
WILLIAM	Thank you very much.
FRANK	The toast is 'Steady the Buffs'.
FIONA	Steady the Buffs?
FRANK	Now then. Let's get down to it. William –
WILLIAM	Er – the –
FRANK	What's that?
WILLIAM	U–bend?
FRANK	Do I?
WILLIAM	No, the one I've come over to look at.
FRANK	Oh, that U–bend. Yes. Well, that's the first thing, William.
WILLIAM	What is?
FRANK	(taking monkey wrench from WILLIAM) There is no U–bend.
WILLIAM	But I thought –
FRANK	I'm afraid you thought wrongly. The U–bend was merely an excuse to get you over here.
WILLIAM	Why?
FIONA	Darling, what is going on?
FRANK	(crossing U.S. of armchair to L. of WILLIAM and putting monkey wrench on table L.) If you will allow me to, I will explain. I'm afraid, William, that what I have to say will come as rather a shock. I'm sorry to say that my wife has been deceiving me – that's why I have asked her

to stay here so that she can tell you about the whole sordid business from start to finish.

FIONA   You can't be serious!

FRANK   Hmm?

FIONA   You expect me calmly to sit here, and tell – William everything?   (She rises to R. of WILLIAM.)   Is that what you're getting at?

FRANK   That's the general idea, yes –

FIONA   And just what are you trying to do – humiliate me?

FIONA   No dear. William has the right to know.

FIONA   William has the right to know? Oh, well then, in that case, invite the postman in. Invite the butcher – if you really want to humiliate me, why not make a real show of it?

FRANK   What's the postman got to do with it?

FIONA   I think this is really sinking very low. I mean, at least if you hit me that would show you cared. Go on! Hit me! Hit me!

FRANK   Have you had a bit of a bang already this morning? Got a bit overheated under the hairdryer or something?

FIONA   (leaning over WILLIAM)   Don't try to be funny with me!

WILLIAM   Pardon, I'm not quite sure –

FIONA   The point is, William, that my husband is trying to tell you, in a rather sordid way, about a very silly, very trivial love affair between Bob Phillips and –   (She turns away from WILLIAM.)

FRANK   And your wife, William. Precisely. I think you could have put it a bit better than that. I was trying to spare the poor chap's feelings.

WILLIAM   My wife?   (He rises.)

FRANK   (pushing WILLIAM down and patting him on the shoulder) Sorry, old chap. You had to know sooner or later.

FIONA   His wife? You mean Mary Featherstone?

FRANK	Of course I mean Mary Featherstone. Only got one wife, hasn't he? I hope.
WILLIAM	My wife and Bob Phillips?
FIONA	Darling, you can't mean it? Bob Phillips and Mary Featherstone?
FRANK	Mary Featherstone and Bob Phillips. I wish everyone wouldn't keep repeating the damn thing –
FIONA	(crossing and sitting L. end of sofa) That's utterly ridiculous –
WILLIAM	I've never heard anything so – absurd –
FRANK	Yes, I know, it must be an absolute wallop in the old bread-basket for you, William, but there it is. (He crosses U.S. of armchair to L. of FIONA.) I don't know why you're sounding so surprised all of a sudden, darling. You've been covering up for the wretched girl for three days –
FIONA	Covering up?
WILLIAM	Absolutely absurd –
FRANK	(turning to WILLIAM) Now let's be totally fair about this, William. You haven't been exactly guiltless yourself, have you? Now, there's not much escapes me, so don't try and deny it. I quite appreciate this is hardly the moment to remind you of your own sorties with those boots of yours and so on –
WILLIAM	Boots?
FRANK	The ones you keep on top of the filing cabinet. I know all about those, too, you see –
WILLIAM	Those are my potholing boots –
FRANK	No, I'm not really interested in what name you choose to call it, William. I just want to deal, perfectly calmly with the facts. Last Wednesday night my wife returned home very late indeed and informed me that she had been spending an evening with Mary. This, I have since discovered, was palpably untrue.
FIONA	Darling, you have got hold of the most –

FRANK	Sssh, please! May I just – This story was an invention of my wife's –
WILLIAM	Was it, Mrs Foster?
FIONA	Well, in a way, yes. But I –
FRANK	You see.
FIONA	But I certainly wasn't covering up for Mary –
FRANK	What other possible reason could you have had for concocting this story? Answer me that?
FIONA	(stumped) Well – er – no – none at all.
FRANK	Precisely. I'm afraid that's definitely minus score as far as I'm concerned, darling. (He crosses U.S. to chair U.S. of table L.)
WILLIAM	But I can't see that that proves –
FRANK	(picking up chair, crossing to L. of WILLIAM, putting down chair and sitting) I am coming to that, William. This morning, I had Teresa Phillips round here. She informed me she had discovered her husband to be having an affair. After she left, I phoned Bob Phillips. I spoke to your wife, William. She was in his house –
WILLIAM	At Bob Phillips! What was she doing at Bob Phillips!
FRANK	I'm trying to spell this out in words of one syllable, William. She answered the phone, pretending, as far as I could judge to be the maid or something. Phillips she informed me was upstairs in the bath. She claimed to be dusting. You can put what interpretation you like on that. To me it only pointed to one thing –
WILLIAM	(dazed, incredulous) I – can't believe this – my wife – ? Is this true, Mrs Foster?
FIONA	I – um – mmmm.
WILLIAM	Of course. That's what you were trying to tell me before your husband came in, wasn't it? How would you react, you said, if you found your wife had been unfaithful to you? And I said –
FIONA	You'd hit her – yes, I remember.

WILLIAM   Yes. Did I say that? Yes, that's right –   (He
               swallows sherry and rises.)

FRANK   (rising)   Now steady, old lad –

WILLIAM   Could I possibly have a drink, please –

FRANK   Yes, of course, of course. What would you like? Bloody
               Mary? No – no –   scotch?   (He crosses U.S. to
               drinks cabinet and pours a scotch.)   Right.

               (WILLIAM crosses to table and picks up monkey wrench
               and crosses U.S. of armchair to C. FIONA leaps up and
               crosses to R. of WILLIAM.)

FIONA   (taking monkey wrench)   William, I really would
               think before you do anything –

               (FRANK crosses D.S. to L. of WILLIAM with drink.)

WILLIAM   Do you realise, Mrs Foster, the hours I've put into that
               woman? When I met her, you know, she was nothing.
               Nothing at all. With my own hands I have built her up.
               Encouraging her to join the public library and make use of
               her non-fiction tickets –   I introduced her to the Concert
               Classics Record Club –   I've coaxed her, encouraged her
               to think – even perhaps bullied her, some might say.
               (He takes drink from FRANK.)   Thank you very much –
               Her dress sense was terrible, my own mother encouraged
               her towards adventurous cooking – everything. I've done
               everything –

FIONA   Jolly good. Cheers.

               (WILLIAM swigs the glass.)

FRANK   Hoy. Steady on.

WILLIAM   And then a man like Phillips – Phillips can come along
               and –   (He crosses U.S. towards double doors.)
               How dare he? How dare he?   (He crosses D.S. and
               bangs glass down on table.)

FRANK   Might be a good idea if you stayed for lunch, William.

WILLIAM   How dare he –   (He crosses U.S. to double doors.)

FIONA   William, dear, do sit down –

               (WILLIAM crosses to FIONA, snatches monkey wrench and

crosses U.S.)

WILLIAM	How dare he – (He rushes out U.L.)
FIONA	Stop him!
FRANK	Too late.
FIONA	Now look what you've done.
FRANK	Me?
FIONA	You realise that man is in a totally unbalanced state. The mood he's in at the moment, he could shoot someone.
FRANK	With a monkey wrench? Do you think that's possible? (He crosses to phone and starts to dial.) I think I'd better call Bob Phillips and warn him –
FIONA	(crossing D.S., picking up chair L. of armchair and placing it L. of double doors) They were perfectly happy until you started on them.
FRANK	Me?
FIONA	Yes.
FRANK	Now look here, I don't think you can really keep on blaming me for this.
FIONA	I'm going to change. (She crosses to doors U.L.) I'm going to get out of this monstrosity. (She exits U.L.)
	(MARY enters from kitchen L. and crosses to front door U.R. FRANK crosses D.S. of armchair with phone. MARY crosses and answers phone.)
MARY	Hallo.
FRANK	Hallo.
MARY	Hallo. Oh hallo, that's Mr Carrycot, isn't it?
FRANK	No. Is that you Mary, now –
MARY	I'm sorry, Mr Carrycot, Mr Phillips is in the bedroom at the moment –
FRANK	Mary –
MARY	His wife is with him, so I didn't like to disturb them –

FRANK   Mary listen to me. This is Foster, do you hear? Foster –

MARY   Who?

FRANK   Frank Foster –

MARY   Oh, I thought you were Mr –

FRANK   Yes, yes quite. But I'm not. I'm me. Now listen, Mary.
               This is urgent. You must replace that receiver and leave
               that house immediately, do you understand?

MARY   Yes. But –

FRANK   Don't argue. Just do as you're told. But before you
               leave you must go upstairs and tell Phillips to lock himself
               in that bedroom and stay there –

MARY   But I can't go in, he's with his wife –

FRANK   This is a matter of life and death, woman. Now Mary,
               when you've done that. Leave the house. But on no
               account go to your home. Come straight round here.
               And run, run, all the way, do you hear? It's vital you do
               this.

MARY   But Mr Foster, I've to get William's dinner. He gets very
               cross –

FRANK   William is more than cross just at the moment, Mary, he's –

WILLIAM   (bursting through front door U.R.)   Mary!

MARY   (looking off to the door)   Oh, talk of the devil, Mr
               Foster. Here he is –

FRANK   Take cover! Take cover!   (He kneels D.S. of
               armchair C.)   Get down on the floor –

MARY   Beg your pardon?

WILLIAM   Mary!   (He crosses to U.S. of sofa.)

MARY   Hallo, William.   (Into receiver.)   Just hold on a
               minute Mr Foster, will you –

FRANK   Mary, Mary – for goodness sake –   (He realises he is
               talking to no one.)   Oh –   (He stands holding the
               receiver anxiously.)

WILLIAM   (crossing R. of sofa and D.S. to R. of MARY)   So, it's

	true, Mary. It's true.
MARY	What?
WILLIAM	I would not have believed this of you, Mary. I would never have believed it. How could you do this? (He brandishes monkey wrench and crosses to table R. and slams monkey wrench down. Loudly.)　　How could you do this?
MARY	You're not cross that I came round, are you William?
FRANK	Mary, can you get hold of a blunt instrument?
WILLIAM	(turning)　　Leave this house! Leave this house, this instant –
MARY	But I'm on the telephone –　　(She starts gnawing her nails.)
WILLIAM	I am warning you, Mary. I am very near to violence. (He crosses to R. of MARY and smacks her hand ineffectively.)　　I have never struck or molested you since the say we were married. Even under these circumstances I do not wish to start. But I shall do so, Mary, I shall do so –　If you do not leave this house –
MARY	I came round because Terry needed help that's all –
WILLIAM	Terry? Is Terry here, too?
MARY	She's in the bedroom with Bob –
WILLIAM	And what sort of help do you intend giving her in there may I ask?
MARY	No. She's having a love affair.
WILLIAM	Who is?
MARY	Terry. With a man from the newspaper.
FRANK	My God, another one.
MARY	(into phone)　　Just a minute, Mr Foster –
FRANK	Mary –
MARY	She writes to him, you see. Bob told me. His name's Mr Carrycot. He's the editor of The Guardian –
WILLIAM	What a feeble, shabby tale.　　(He advances on her.)

You deceitful slut!

FRANK   Hallo!

(BOB in his dressing gown enters from bedroom L. and crosses to U.S. of sofa. WILLIAM crosses to R. of BOB.)

BOB   Look, I'd be grateful if you two would take your domestic quarrels elsewhere –

(WILLIAM leaps forward and swings a blow at BOB. It goes low and catches him in the stomach.)

WILLIAM   You swine, Phillips. You swine –

BOB   (collapsing on his knees with a grunt)   Aagh!

WILLIAM   That'll teach you!

MARY   William!

WILLIAM   (crossing to R. of sofa nursing his hand)   That'll teach you!

FRANK   Hallo! Hallo!

FIONA   (entering U.L.)   Hallo.   (She crosses D.S. to L. of FRANK.)

FRANK   Get down on the floor dear.

FIONA   (kneeling L. of FRANK)   Darling, what's the matter?

FRANK   Something going on. No shots yet, thank God, but –

WILLIAM   If you get up, I shall hit you again, Phillips. I warn you.

BOB   (rising U.S. of sofa)   What the hell was that in aid of –

MARY   William, are you alright?

FIONA   Darling are you alright?

WILLIAM   I'm alright.

FRANK   I'm alright.

WILLIAM   I'm the only one in this house that is alright –

BOB   (crossing to R. of sofa, L. of WILLIAM)   What's he on about, Mary? Gone off his rocker has he?   (He rises to his feet.)

(TERESA enters in a housecoat from L. WILLIAM springs forward again and hits BOB in the eye this time. BOB collapses backwards onto sofa. MARY still holding the phone - screams. FRANK who gets this down the telephone - yells and jumps back. FIONA reacting to this - cries out. WILLIAM's impetus from the blow he has landed BOB sends him, doubled up, past BOB and almost careering into TERESA. She, with a swift, two-handed blow on the back of his neck, floors WILLIAM completely. MARY drops phone and exits screaming U.R. TERESA tends to BOB. Almost immediately MARY enters U.L. through FRANK's front door, still screaming. FIONA and FRANK, who is still shouting advice to MARY down the phone, rise in amazement. MARY crosses D.S., L. of armchair C. to between FRANK and FIONA.)

MARY   I - I - I - aaaah.   (She falls in a dead faint.)

CURTAIN

Scene Two

Set as in Act I, Scene 1 except all three seats of settee now match FOSTER's decor.

Sunday morning.

          (FRANK paces up and down C.S., U.S. of armchair C.)

FRANK   Fellow workers -   Members of my department -   Let's put our cards on the table -

FIONA   (entering from kitchen R. with two cups and crossing to R. of FRANK)   Coffee?

FRANK   Just one cup -

          (FIONA gives FRANK coffee.)

Oh, thank you.

FIONA   (crossing and sitting in armchair C.)   Are you sure this is the right thing?

FRANK   Absolutely.

FIONA   But it really has nothing to do with us.

FRANK   They're all members of my department. As such I feel their physical and, to a certain extent, spiritual welfare are my concern.

FIONA   Oh, darling, that's dreadfully pompous.

FRANK   There is nothing pompous about human concern. I wonder if you'd mind not sitting there.

(FIONA rises and crosses and sits C. of sofa.)

(sitting in armchair C.)   Thank you. Where's Mary?

FIONA   I've only just woken her. She had a nice long sleep. The best thing for her.

FRANK   As long as she's down for the meeting –

FIONA   She'll be down. Probably starving as well. She ate nothing last night. Not a bite.

(The doorbell rings.)

FRANK   That'll be the Phillips.

(FRANK and FIONA rise.)

FIONA   (crossing U.S. to double doors)   I'll let them in. This isn't going to take too long, I trust. I've put newspaper down in the hall, so their baby can spill anything it likes –   (She goes out.)

(FRANK crosses to U.L. of armchair and paces about.)

FRANK   (muttering)   Team mates – a team that plays together stays together, but some of us have been playing too hard –   (He crosses to U.L. of sofa.)   I expect some of you are wondering why I –

(TERESA, FIONA and BOB enter U.L. to D.S. of steps.)

FIONA   Here we are.

FRANK	(shaking all three of them by the hand) Come in. Come in. Come in.
TERESA	Hallo, Frank.
BOB	Hi Frank.
FRANK	Do sit down. Sit down. Sit down.

(TERESA crosses and sits L. end of sofa. BOB crosses and sits in armchair C. FIONA crosses to double doors.)

(crossing to R. of armchair)   Now, I've asked you here –

FIONA	(calling) Mary!
BOB	What's it all about?
FRANK	Well, I've asked you –
FIONA	(crossing R. and going out into kitchen R.) I'll bring you some coffee. (She goes out.)
FRANK	I've asked – (He notices BOB's bruised face.) That's a nasty knock, Bob. Where'd you get that?
BOB	That's an interesting story, actually –
TERESA	William did it –
FRANK	William? I see.
BOB	More than we do.
FRANK	Exactly. I wonder if you'd mind not sitting –

(BOB rises and crosses and sits C. of sofa.)

(crossing D.S. of armchair)   Thank you. Now, the idea of this morning is to try and undo some of the damage –

(FIONA enters from kitchen R. with coffee tray with four cups and puts it down on table L.)

FIONA	Coffee? Bob? Terry?
BOB	Thanks.
TERESA	Thank you.

(FIONA pours coffee.)

FRANK	The point is, Terry –
FIONA	Terry, white?
TERESA	Please.
FRANK	Terry –
FIONA	Sugar?
TERESA	Two, please.
	(FIONA hands TERESA coffee.)
FRANK	Terry! Let's keep calm, shall we? I did warn you on the phone that we may be in for some nasty shocks –
FIONA	You're both looking terribly well –
TERESA	Are we?
FIONA	I love your bruise, Bob – How did you get it?
BOB	Oh, I – picked it up fairly cheaply somewhere –
FIONA	(handing BOB coffee) Suits you. I should keep it. (She crosses to U.S. of sofa.)
FRANK	I really must insist that we keep to the subject. We have a lot to get through this morning –
BOB	This has the air of a rather seedy annual general meeting. Where exactly do Terry and I come into it?
FRANK	That's a pretty cynical thing to say, Bob. Considering.
TERESA	Oh, what have you been doing now?
BOB	Me?
TERESA	Yes.
BOB	Nothing.
FRANK	Will you please address your remarks through the chair. Now, Bob, before Mary comes down, and before William gets here –
BOB	(jumping up) William!
FRANK	Oh, do sit down, Bob.
BOB	I'm not staying here. That man's unbalanced.

FRANK   I wouldn't go so far as to say unbalanced.

             (FIONA crosses to U.S. of armchair C. and perches on
             back of chair.)

             I agree it was a rather drastic course of action to take,
             but understandable, under the circumstances.

BOB   Oh, perfectly understandable. He's off his nut, that's
             all.   (He sits.)

FRANK   Darling would you mind not -

             (FIONA crosses to U.S. of sofa.)

             Now before Mary comes down, and before -

             (MARY enters U.L. onto steps. FIONA crosses U.S. to
             D.R. of MARY D.S. of steps.)

FIONA   Ah. Here she is.

             (MARY crosses D.S., L. of armchair.)

             (crossing to U.S. of sofa)   Mary, come in and sit
             down -

MARY   Hallo.

TERESA   Hallo, Mary.

             (MARY sits in armchair C.)

FRANK   No, not there, Mary, please!

             (MARY leaps up and crosses to sofa. BOB moves to R. end
             and MARY sits C.)

FIONA   Coffee, Mary?

MARY   Thank you.

             (FIONA pours coffee.)

FRANK   I was just saying, Mary, that the reason we're all here is
             that we want to try and put things right for you.

FIONA   (handing MARY coffee)   Mary -

MARY   Thank you.

FRANK   Not at all. The point is, that when William arrives -

MARY   (jumping up) William! Oh no -

FRANK	Oh, do sit down, Mary.
	(MARY sits.)
	You're quite safe.
MARY	I don't think I can –
FRANK	When William arrives, you must be quite straight and honest with him. Don't try and pretend it's anything less than it is – a love affair – a perfectly ordinary love affair between yourself and Bob Phillips.
MARY	A what?
BOB	Eh?
TERESA	What?
FRANK	(a bit startled by their reaction crossing D.C.) Well, those are the facts, aren't they?
BOB	Frank. You must be joking.
FRANK	Hardly a subject for – mirth, I'd have thought –
MARY	I haven't had an affair with Bob – honestly, Terry.
TERESA	(laughing) No, I do believe you.
FRANK	Well, in that case I – are you sure you haven't?
BOB	Where the hell did you get that idea –
FRANK	Um. Well, it came in dribs and drabs, really.
BOB	I see.
FRANK	Oh, well, if you haven't had an affair, we'll have to change the agenda. (He crosses D.L.) It certainly makes things a lot simpler –
	(The doorbell rings. MARY jumps up. TERESA pulls her down.)
MARY	William!
FIONA	Oh Lord. (She goes to answer the door U.L.)
BOB	Is that why he hit me?
FRANK	Presumably.
BOB	It's always nice to know – When one is struck down in

one's own sitting room –

TERESA	You'd be a fat lot of good in a crisis. You didn't even put up a fight.
BOB	I didn't know there was a fight –

(WILLIAM enters U.L. and crosses D.S. to R. of FRANK. FIONA enters U.L. and crosses to U.L. of sofa.)

WILLIAM	I came as quickly as I could. I don't know much about immersion heaters but I'll see what – Oh. (He glares at the assembled company.)
FRANK	Ah, William.
BOB	Hallo.
WILLIAM	Is this some sort of humorous prank?
FRANK	William –
WILLIAM	Not very amusing at all. Inviting me here and then confronting me with him and her – Do you think I want to sit down in the same room as them –
FRANK	William –
WILLIAM	I still have a blinding headache, and I have been up half the night with one – I came round here in good faith to have a look at the thermostat on your immersion heater – as you requested –
FRANK	William!
BOB	(startled) Uh? Yes?
FRANK	There's been a misunderstanding, William.
BOB	You could call it that –
FRANK	The point is – er – I think I misinformed you –
WILLIAM	What about?
BOB	About Mary and me.
FRANK	My information was inaccurate. (He crosses U.S. to U.L. of armchair C.)
WILLIAM	You mean – ?

(BOB shakes his head, then MARY shakes her head.)

WILLIAM   I see.

FIONA   (crossing D.S. to C.)   I suggest, William, the very
               best thing you can do is to take Mary home and have a
               lovely lunch together and then you can both kiss and
               make up - I'll see you all out.   (She crosses U.S. to
               double doors.)

               (BOB and TERESA rise. TERESA crosses to D.L. of steps
               and BOB crosses U.S. of sofa to U.L. corner of sofa.)

WILLIAM   (crossing to D.S. of armchair)   Well, I don't quite
               know what to say. I've been badly misled.

BOB   (crossing D.S. to R. of WILLIAM)   You should have
               checked your facts first, shouldn't you?

WILLIAM   Well - I'm sorry, Bob. I - er - I hope you weren't too
               badly hurt?

BOB   Not too badly, at all. Short spell in the iron lung and
               I'll be fine.

TERESA   (crossing D.S. to L. of WILLIAM)   How's your head?

WILLIAM   Not so bad, I -

TERESA   Sorry about that, too.

WILLIAM   No, no. My fault entirely.

               (BOB and TERESA cross U.S. to steps.)

               Well, I think the best thing is for us both to leave now -
               rather than -

FIONA   You haven't had coffee?

WILLIAM   No, no thank you, Mrs Foster.

               (FIONA crosses to R. of steps.)

               Mary?

MARY   Yes?

WILLIAM   Come along.   (He crosses U.S. to steps, between BOB
               and TERESA.)

MARY   Just a minute -

               (WILLIAM, TERESA, BOB and FIONA turn to MARY.)

WILLIAM   Yes?

MARY   What about me? You've apologised to everyone else, what about me - ?

WILLIAM   I don't have to apologise to you. I was misled.

MARY   How?

WILLIAM   (crossing D.S. to U.L. of sofa)   Surely you've grasped the situation. I was told -

MARY   You've always told me, never believe everything people tell you -

WILLIAM   True, but -

MARY   Then why did you?

WILLIAM   That's an entirely different - Mr Foster told me -

MARY   I want an apology -

            (FIONA, BOB and TERESA cross D.S.)

WILLIAM   (crossing to L. of sofa)   Mary, don't start a scene here -

MARY   I'm not leaving here till I get an apology -

WILLIAM   Darling, I shall get angry.

BOB   (crossing to U.S. of sofa)   Go on - apologise.

WILLIAM   Do you mind?

            (TERESA crosses to U.L. of armchair. FIONA crosses to U.L. of sofa.)

TERESA   I think you owe her an apology, William -

WILLIAM   Thank you very much, Terry, I'll deal with my own affairs -

FRANK   I'd apologise if I were you, old chap. Much the easiest thing to do -

WILLIAM   Oh. Well - if you say so, Mr Foster -

FRANK   Decent thing to do.

WILLIAM   In that case I'm - I'm - I'm -   (He can't say it.)

MARY   That'll do.   (She rises and crosses L., D.S. of

armchair and shakes FRANK's hand, and crosses R., U.S.
of armchair and shakes FIONA's hand and crosses into
doorway U.L.)   Thank you. We'll go now. Thank
you very much, Mr Foster, Mrs Foster for looking after
me –

FIONA   A pleasure.

FRANK   Goodbye, Mary – Best of luck –

MARY   Thank you. William?

(WILLIAM steps forward. He continues spluttering and
gesticulating for some moments but is unable to anything.
Finally –)

WILLIAM   Cheerio.   (He stalks out U.L.)

(MARY turns after him and turns back.)

MARY   (in a low voice, indicating the departed WILLIAM)
It's difficult for him. He's never been wrong before, you
see.   (She exits U.L.)

(FIONA follows MARY. TERESA crosses and shakes
FRANK's hand. FIONA reappears in doorway.)

FIONA   Oh, Terry, your baby appears to be eating all that
newspaper I put down for him, in the hall. Is it good for
him?

TERESA   Depends which one.   (She exits U.L.)

(FIONA follows TERESA. BOB crosses L. and FRANK
crosses R. and they meet and shake hands D.S. of steps.)

FRANK   Er – Just one word of warning, Bob.

BOB   What?

FRANK   Well, when Mary was here last night, couldn't get much
out of her, but she did say something, I think you ought to
know – Apparently, Terry might be getting herself
involved with some – newspaper man –

BOB   Newspaper man?

FRANK   Yes, apparently –

BOB   You mean one of those blokes who stand on corners
shouting –

FRANK   No, no. Journalist chap –

BOB   Oh. Really? Thanks –

FRANK   Just watch out.

BOB   (puzzled)   Yes, right. Cheerio then.   (He exits
            U.L.)

            (FRANK crosses and sits L. end of sofa.)

FRANK   (rubbing his hands together, pleased)   Good, good,
            good –

FIONA   (entering U.L., crossing to table L. and beginning to
            stack cups)   Well done, darling.

FRANK   A good morning's work, I think. Good morning's work.

FIONA   (crossing D.S., R. of sofa, collecting cups from coffee
            table and then crossing U.S. to table L.)   That really
            is the most awful baby they have. Quite apart from
            looking like an unsuccessful Hogarth, it's left a large
            damp patch on our carpet again. Have to leave the front
            door open – let it dry out –

FRANK   (thoughtful suddenly)   Just a minute. There's
            something missing. There's a loose end somewhere –

FIONA   (crossing to L. of FRANK and taking cup)   Yes, well,
            don't you worry about that now. You spend much too
            much time worrying about other people's problems –
            (She crosses U.S. to table L.)

FRANK   You told me, first, that you were out with Mary on
            Wednesday last –

FIONA   Did I?

FRANK   Yes. Then you said, under pressure – No, I was just
            covering up for Mary, didn't you –

FIONA   Yes, possibly.

FRANK   However, since Mary was not having an affair, you
            wouldn't have needed to cover up for her, would you?

FIONA   I suppose not –

FRANK   No. You wouldn't – So the question remains – What on
            earth were you up to on Wednesday night – ?

FIONA	Oh, I was – pottering about, you know –
FRANK	Been behaving rather peculiarly lately, altogether.
FIONA	Really?
FRANK	Yes.
FIONA	Good. (She picks up tray and turns towards kitchen.) More coffee?
FRANK	Where were you?
FIONA	(laughing) You don't really want to know – do you?
FRANK	Yes, I do.
FIONA	Oh. (Pause. She puts tray down and crosses to L. of sofa.) Well. Well, I did something rather – silly.
FRANK	Did you?
FIONA	Yes. (Pause.) Are you going to be awfully cross with me?
FRANK	No.
FIONA	Well, we sort of met and then we –
FRANK	Another chap.
FIONA	Yes.
FRANK	Oh.
FIONA	It really wasn't anything.
FRANK	No. Do I know him?
FIONA	Sort of.
FRANK	I see.
FIONA	It really wasn't – I mean – nothing – He wasn't half as nice as you.
FRANK	Oh.
FIONA	(kneeling L. of FRANK and putting arms round his neck) Are you going to forgive me?
FRANK	Yes, of course. I mean, nothing much else I can do, is there? So long as you don't make a sort of habit of it –

FIONA   (kissing him on forehead)   Darling –

FRANK   Hmmmm.

FIONA   I'll tell you what. I'll make us a special un-anniversary dinner to make up for it. Something nice. And you can open a bottle of wine and we'll have a squiffy evening together. What about that?

FRANK   Um?

FIONA   I know, I'll put on some of that delicious perfume you bought me after lunch, shall I?

FRANK   Oh, yes. Do that!

FIONA   (rising, crossing to table L., picking up tray and crossing towards kitchen)   Good.

FRANK   Fiona? Who was it?

FIONA   Who?

FRANK   This man you – ?

FIONA   Oh. No one of the least importance –

FRANK   Someone we know, though – ?

FIONA   It really doesn't matter –   (She exits into kitchen R.)

FRANK   (muttering)   Someone we know – ?   (He rises, takes phone pad from table R. of C. chair and crosses and sits L. end of sofa. He thumbs through phone pad.)

          (BOB enters U.R. and crosses L. and exits into kitchen L.)

          Adams – no, Atkinson – Aubrey S – who's Aubrey S? Oh him – No – Associated Dairies – no –   (He continues to mutter.)

          (TERESA enters U.R. and crosses D.S. BOB enters from kitchen L. and crosses to L. of TERESA and hands her cigarette.)

TERESA   What a waste of a morning.

          (BOB crosses and sits in armchair D.L. TERESA crosses to his R.)

BOB   I'm sure Frank enjoyed it –

TERESA   (laughing)   You and Mary Featherstone – I'd love to
                have seen that –

BOB   I don't know how the hell Frank got hold of that idea –

                (They laugh.)

TERESA   Well. Now if he'd said you and Fiona – ?

                (BOB stops laughing.)

                Is it over between you two?

BOB   What?

TERESA   It was pretty obvious.

BOB   Oh.

                (Pause.)

TERESA   Well, if it had to be someone, I'd sooner her than Mary –

BOB   So would I.

TERESA   No, I mean, Mary's a sticker. If she took a fancy to you,
                she'd hang on. Fiona knows which side her bread is
                buttered.   (She goes out into the kitchen L.)

FRANK   Yates – Yeoman – YMCA –

                (TERESA enters from kitchen and crosses to R. of BOB
                with perfume.)

BOB   What's that?

TERESA   Bottle of perfume. I noticed it on the hall table at
                Fiona's. Benjy must have reached out of his carry-cot
                and taken it –

BOB   Oh, yes?

TERESA   Quite nice. I think I'll keep it. I think she owes it to
                me.   (She crosses D.S. of sofa to table R. and sits at
                U.S. end of table.)   I can't think what you saw in
                her – apart from promotion.

BOB   Come on. What about you?

TERESA   Me?

BOB   Your friend. The journalist.

TERESA	Journalist?
BOB	I've heard.
TERESA	I don't know any journalists.
BOB	No?
TERESA	No. I wish I did. You know, you were a fool to do it. Frank's bound to find out sooner or later.
FRANK	Someone we – ah! Good Lord! Good Lord, yes! Of course. (He stands for a moment staring at the door as the realization dawns, then goes to the phone and dials.)
	(BOB rises and crosses U.S. towards kitchen L.)
TERESA	Where are you going?
BOB	(dignified) I'm going to get the lunch.
TERESA	You're what?
BOB	I'm going to get the bloody lunch. What's wrong with that? (He goes into the kitchen.)
TERESA	My God!
	(After a long pause, TERESA's phone rings. FRANK is growling menacingly into the phone. TERESA advances, warily, and picks up the phone, and hears FRANK growling.)
	That's screwdriver, isn't it?
FRANK	Screwdriver?
TERESA	Oh, good, you're talking. That's a great step forward. Now listen to me. Does it give you some sort of kick phoning up women and trying to frighten them? Does it?
FRANK	Er – no – not really. I don't think so. I don't really know.
TERESA	Look. You obviously need help. Haven't you anyone you can talk to – a wife or a mother –
FRANK	Mummy's passed away.
BOB	(entering from kitchen L. and crossing U.S. to R. of

TERESA)   Where the hell are all the saucepans?
(He has an apron on.)

TERESA   (to BOB)   Sssh!

(FIONA enters from kitchen R. and crosses U.S. to L. of
FRANK.)

FRANK   (as FIONA enters, misinterpreting, whispers)   – and
my wife's in the kitchen –

FIONA   What's that?

FRANK   (to FIONA)   Sssh!

TERESA   Look, I'm sorry to sound technical, but – are you – very
frustrated?

BOB   Eh?

TERESA   Sssh!

FRANK   Frustrated?

TERESA   You know. Sexually.

FRANK   Sexually?

FIONA   Sexually?!

FRANK   Sssh!

TERESA   Look. I can't talk any more now, but if you want to –
ring me up again and we can even meet somewhere and
have a session.

FRANK   Meet somewhere – yes – that'd be nice –

TERESA   Good. Well, now that you've got my number, call me up
any time you want me.

FRANK   Thank you very much. I'll do that. Goodbye.

TERESA   Goodbye.

(FRANK and TERESA put down phones.)

BOB   Who was that?

FIONA   Who was that?

TERESA   (pleased)   No one you know.

FRANK   Just a boy I was at school with, dear.

CURTAIN

FURNITURE AND PROPERTY PLOT

ACT I Scene 1

SET

D.R. Dining table (P)
  On it
    Newspaper cuttings
    Letters
    Old newspapers
    Files
    Scissors
    Transistor radio
    Box of tissues
  Under it
    Telephone directory
  Two dining chairs (P)
    On chair D.S. of table
    BOB's jacket with £5
    note in pocket
  Full wastepaper basket (P)

D.R.C. Three-seater settee
    R. two seats (F)
    L. seat (P)

U.R. Shelves to L. and R. of
    front door (P)
    On them
      Clutter of books, files,
      toys, etc.
    Near door
      Pegs with coats on them
      (P)
    Welsh dresser (P)
    On it
      Tin tray
      Cigarettes
      Matches
      Tumbler containing
      pencils
      Candle on plate
      Plates
      Similar clutter to that
      on shelves

Small table (P)
  On it
    Vase of flowers

U.L. Drinks cabinet (F) – to R. of
    front doors (F)
    On it
      Silver tray
      Whisky decanter (full)
      Two sherry decanters (full)
      Two whisky tumblers
      Six sherry glasses
      Bottle opener
    In it
      Gin
      Martini
      Orange juice
      Tonic water
      Ginger ale
      Soda water
      Spare bottle opener
    Small table (F) – to L. of
    front doors (F)
    On it
      Vase of flowers

C. Armchair (F)
    Small table (F) to R. of
    armchair

D.C. Composite coffee table (F
    and P) L. section (P)
    On it
      Telephone
      Ashtray
      Notepad
      Pencil
      Dishcloth
    R. section (F)
    On it
      Telephone
      Notepad
      Pencil
      Eggtimer

FURNITURE AND PROPERTY PLOT

Transistor radio
T.V. Times
Wastepaper basket (F)

L.   Dining table (F)
Two dining chairs (F)

D.L.   Armchair (P)
Over back
apron
Child's playpen (P)
In it
Various toys
Baby walker (P)
Baby chair (P)
Doll's house (P)
In it
BOB's shoe with toy
squeaker in toe

OFFSTAGE

R.   In kitchen (F)
Tray
On it
Two cups
Two saucers
Two spoons
Two small plates
Two napkins
Two knives
Salt cellar
Butter dish with butter
Sugar bowl with
sugar lumps
Marmalade pot
Marmalade spoon
Silver coffee pot with
coffee
Silver milk jug with
milk
Toast rack with toast
Egg cup with boiled egg
Shoe-box

Electric toothbrush
Screwdriver

U.R.   Outside front door (P)
Newspaper (Guardian)

U.L.   Outside front doors (F)
Newspapers
Small parcel containing
perfume
Hat   )
Coat   )
Umbrella) FRANK
Briefcase)

L.   In kitchen and bedroom
section (P)
Mug of tea
Plate with sandwich
Newspaper (Guardian)
Large spoon
One black shoe
One brown shoe
Blue file
Boxes

PERSONAL

FIONA   Watch
TERESA Mug of tea
FRANK   Watch

ACT I Scene 2

STRIKE Coffee tables
Wastepaper baskets
Things on D.R. dining
table (P)
Coffee mugs
Newspapers
Flowers from U.R. small
table (P)

Wrapping from perfume (P)

FURNITURE AND PROPERTY PLOT

MOVE   D.R. dining table and two chairs (P) to C.
L. dining table and two chairs (F) to C.
C. chair (F) to U.R.
C. small table (F) to D.S. of settee
U.R. small table (P) D.S.R. of dining tables

U.C.   Two swivel chairs

U.L.   Trolley (F)

U.R.   Pile of nappies

All three seats of settee (F)

C.   Dining table (F)
     At each place
       Table mat
       Two knives
       Three forks
       Dessert spoon
       Small spoon
       Side plate
     Cruet set
     Mat for serving dish
     Two candelabras with candles
Dining table (P)
     At each place
       Table mat
       Knife
       Fork
       Spoon
       Small plate
       Soup dish
     Mat for serving dish
     Salt and pepper
     Bottle of white wine
     Corkscrew

OFFSTAGE

R.   In kitchen (F)
Tray with glasses and napkins
FRANK's shoes
Four dishes of avocado
Bottle of wine
Two vegetable dishes
Dish of frigadella
Four dinner plates

U.R.   Outside front door (P)
Carrier bag with tins of beer

L.   In kitchen and bedroom (P)
Tray with three tumblers and a packet of paper napkins
Mug of tea
Wet nappy
Tureen of soup with ladle

PERSONAL

FRANK   Newspaper
BOB   Newspaper
WILLIAM   Coat
           Hat
MARY   Gloves
           Cardigan
           Coat

ACT II Scene 1

STRIKE   All dinner cutlery, etc.
Two swivel chairs
Trolley (F)

SET

Wash whisky and sherry glasses (F) and replace on drinks cabinet

Reset all furniture as in Act I